REALIZE YOUR POTENTIAL

REALIZE YOUR POTENTIAL

Robert J. McKain, Jr.

amacom A DIVISION OF AMERICAN MANAGEMENT ASSOCIATIONS

Library of Congress Cataloging in Publication Data

McKain, Robert J
    Realize your potential.

    1. Success. I. Title.
HF5386.M196   650'.1   75-14418
ISBN 0-8144-5380-5

First Printing

Foreword

Realize Your Potential by Robert J. McKain, Jr., is an unusual, penetrating, creative, and constructive approach to and analysis of the life of the individual in the modern complex business world.

It is unusually structured in its approach to the depths and mystiques of the human personality.

It is obviously written by an individual with unique experience and insights.

Men and women over a wide range of activities, status, and objectives will find it well worth reading.

HAROLD E. STASSEN

Preface

This book is about the dignity, self-respect, and potential of a businessman, whether he is the chief executive officer of a corporation or a junior executive or salesman. The continued development of self-respect and the use of potential is a never-ending quest for any man in business, and cannot be taken for granted. The business of Watergate illustrates dramatically that the highest office in the land is no guarantee of a permanent state of achievement or contentment.

The opportunities lost through the nonuse of potential are of vital concern to the corporations in this country. By virtue of sheer size a company can, to some degree, average out the potential factor, but that's not so with an individual man. The ways in which he uses his many potentials affect his entire life. He can be fulfilled, just slightly miserable, or lead a "life of quiet desperation." Yet the differences among three men with these three different life patterns can often be rather small.

This book is directed to the man who wants to grow and to motivate himself. It is not about the role the corporation might play in the development effort. This should be left to the Peter Druckers and others who are skilled in these areas. Rather, the emphasis here is on the search by the individual businessman to realize himself, to fulfill himself. For that reason, the discussions are oriented to business potential because it is within that area that the factors involved in potential development can be more readily isolated. But in addition to that objective, the aim is to help the individual to realize his *total* potential so that he enriches his life each day that he lives and in all aspects of his life.

Although many business principles are used in this book as guides for the development of potential, and therefore involve compensation, these essays are directed to the man who wants to grow and who wants to learn how to motivate himself. He should realize that the word "potential" is a broad-based term involving all the characteristics of a person and his uniqueness, and including capacities and abilities not related to money. As the reader progresses from chapter to chapter, this will become more apparent to him, for each chapter is a part of every other one, and in some cases the same subject is briefly discussed in several chapters but from a different point of view.

Perhaps it should be noted here that the term "businessman" and the pronoun "he" are used in this book in the context of "businesswoman" as well. The problems and potential of women, who are increasingly choosing important business careers, are of course the same as those of their male counterparts. For the sake of simplicity, however, the male gender is used throughout the discussions.

The material presented comes from the fields of philosophy, religion, psychology, and the realities of competitive business. A broad brush is used in areas that can be very detailed, but my purpose is not the detail but the meaning and practical use of a man's potential. I leave you to judge whether I have captured at least some of the essence and the beauty and the productivity realized by the development of man's potential.

ROBERT J. McKAIN, JR.

Contents

Introduction

An explosive and dynamic search under way today by men in the business world involves the productive use of people in ways that are fulfilling and satisfying to them. The idea of profit, of last year plus 10 percent, as the ultimate goal of business, is being increasingly challenged. While a profitable and growing business is essential—indeed, is the sine qua non of business life—the measurement of human progress everlastingly in monetary terms often places the human growth factor as exclusively associated with the role of second-class citizen. Is the emphasis to be put primarily on the end result—money or what it will buy—or should the primary thrust be toward the growth and the development of the potential of men? It is my belief that a policy predicated on the development of the potential of a company's men is the foundation for the productive effort that will most likely produce the maximum to stockholders, the public, and the employees. Such a policy places the growth of the individual businessman at the base of productivity. It utilizes objectives and goals in terms of individual potential. Its root question is not, "How can we increase profits by 10 percent?" but "How can we help this man to grow?" A corporate or individual program based on helping and growth develops the money necessary to business goals, but in addition makes possible the sense of inner worth and desire to grow which is crucial to creativity and increased individual productivity.

1

Regardless of the wholehearted participation of a company in such guidance plans, a fruitful program cannot be developed as a one-way street. The individual employee must also be dedicated to its purpose. But a major problem arises when a man tries to isolate the attitudes or viewpoints or unused potentials that may be affecting his life. Once most men marry and start to work, their lives are in a sense programmed and they institutionalize their life-style. For some businessmen this is a sufficiently rewarding adventure, but for others it may be an essentially unsatisfying experience. The question is being increasingly asked, "Why?" Why should the individual seek to improve himself?

One of the most able and inspiring managers of men that I have ever known expressed a little of his philosophy when he told me many years ago, "You know, I have never fired a man. If a man is not living up to his potential, and after we've talked about it over a period time, I call him in and tell him with the utmost sincerity, 'Look, Fred, you have great potential which I am unable to get you to use. I'm failing you because there are men who can bring out the best in you. I honestly feel that you should find that man.' " The remarkable part of this story is that even when this manager was in the midst of one of the most difficult parts of business life, his mind was on the potential of the individual. For this was the very reason he was able to increase to an extraordinarily high level the productivity of the men he managed. He never expected more than a man had to give, but his message was clear, "Grow, fulfill yourself, for that's what it's all about. Anything less is a disservice to you." In discussing this with a very competent executive, he said, "You know, most people are searching for answers and there's nothing wrong with searching. But some men are afraid to talk about it because they think that people will feel they are weak and that they don't have it all together. Because they're afraid to talk, their problem becomes worse. Realistically, a degree of dissatisfaction is fundamental to growth. For example, we don't eat unless we're hungry, and we don't go to bed unless we're tired. It's only when we won't recognize that we need something that we have a problem."

In a recent AMA survey of executive productivity, with 1,275 replies from a questionnaire sent to managers and presidents of American business, the authors said, "The executives in this survey want to commit themselves to working in more productive ways. They challenge us to forget the grandiose notion that managers naturally manage properly. We executives—from middle managers to presidents—need all the help we can get."

For years I have been talking to businessmen at all levels about their goals and dreams for their businesses, their families, and their own futures. Most of these goals have been related to money—money to pay taxes, to support the family, to educate children, to live comfortably at retirement. A few years ago I began to ask men how they personally felt about what they were doing and where they wanted to go. The answers were many and varied, but I did not find any man who was satisfied if he thought his work was mediocre. Out of these conversations, I came to the conclusion that the most unexplored resource in this country today is the unused potential of its people.

As a particular matter, relatively few people even begin to utilize their potential to live fully in the present moment, and experts say that occurs because we use only about 5 to 10 percent of the actual capacity of our minds. The future holds great promise of development in this area, about which we can only speculate, but in the meantime we must do what we can with the tools available today.

In thinking about our potential for enjoying life and for earning an income, it almost seems as if there are two different worlds, the business world and the field of human behavior. The business world uses extensively the techniques of planning that leave little to chance, and every known method is used to motivate people and to increase production results. Goals are set and reset, and progress in the direction of those goals is tracked. The ability to measure work potential in terms of money also provides important clues to the realization of potential in the other areas of life. However, once one leaves the business world and enters into those parts of life which are unrelated to money, there is little discussion of goals, of personal planning, of tracking progress, and of achievement generally. At this point, the psychologist and the psychiatrist step in and discuss human behavior in terms of what we think of ourselves, of our ability to love, and of our capacity to grow, or perhaps probe the impact of our parents on our lives. Much of the information developed in this field is of a generalized nature, and is extremely difficult for a person to apply to his own life. But there are those people who seem to get the most out of their activities. They represent a blending of certain desirable physical and mental qualities which are admired by all of us. Through personal development and the coordination of mind and body, they reach most desirable levels of performance in both their work and private lives. These unusual people display certain characteristics that are basic to the principles for realizing potential. All can be explained from the viewpoints of psychology and business, and are fundamental to the approach described in this book.

Contemporary literature on the subject of human behavior generally will offer a person a better understanding of himself. He will learn that his feelings of inferiority are false and are largely based on childhood feelings; that he is a unique individual who should respect himself; that he has the capacity to change for the better; that he should think positively. A person who is seriously thinking about himself, his progress in his work and his life, may reach a stage where he thinks: "What do I do next?" Up to that point he probably has had to work out his own program—and less than 10 percent of the population appears to be able to do so effectively. The remaining 90 percent work with the problem for a while and then give up.

Increasingly, the maturing generation is talking about

its problems, and is searching and reading and trying to find solutions to those problems. To some extent the search has begun to develop in the right place, within the individual himself rather than in external circumstances. People are beginning to understand that to alter the direction in which one is moving is a profound change that involves attitudes and thought processes, and that often this change is needed because they are operating well below their capacity.

Money as a true measure of potential is not a universal yardstick, for a wealthy man may be in trouble, but a shoemaker may have found purpose and meaning to his life and be a truly happy man. On the other hand, money as a measure of a specific potential is valuable in attempting to develop a hypothesis for the development of potential generally, which could then hopefully enable a man to answer his own questions: What's next? What is my potential?

Potential is scored on the scale of 0 to 10, with zero being its nonuse by an individual and 10 its maximum use. Its base is not statistical in nature. It is, rather, a judgment made by an individual to compare his present performance, both vertically (in his work) and horizontally (in his other activities), to his capacity to perform if he went "all out," as he views it, in a given activity. Thus, a score of 8 would indicate a high degree of satisfaction with present performance as well as the knowledge that perfection had not been reached. Many true situations are set forth in this book, although names and places are omitted because of the personal nature of the conversations. The scores mentioned have proved to be most important in the way the individual feels about himself and his work, and have indicated his high capability of growing and using his potential in the future.

Usually it will be found that successful people work constantly at the job of developing and retaining their abilities. Take, for example, a question asked recently in a Miami newspaper: "What's with the envelope that pro golfer Johnny Miller keeps looking at during tournament play on TV?" The answer was, "the blonde bomber keeps golf notes to himself on that brown envelope, such as 'you must keep the head still,' and 'take the club back slowly.' " "It sounds corny," the 26-year-old Miller said, "but each of the sayings serves a purpose. If you keep feeding things to the brain, it remembers and transfers them to the body." Even the finest professional must constantly return to the basics.

In a sense, many parts of this book are "corny," but in any endeavor a man has to constantly return to fundamentals. Miller's notes were reminders to "keep the head still," and to "take the club back slowly," in a sense a feedback of knowledge already acquired. So, too, are the basic checkpoints involved in the process of realizing potential. Without reminders, they can be easily forgotten, and even a slight deviation can detract materially from one's success and enjoyment of life.

1

The process of realizing potential

Recently in the course of a conversation I told a friend about this book and the fact that it dealt with potential. I then asked him how he felt about the use of his own potential in his work and his life. He said, "You know, I have two businesses. One I own and manage; the other is entirely sales. My income is approximately $100,000 per year, and yet in spite of this, I don't feel good about my life, but I don't know what to do. Tell me what to do."

I was taken aback by the meaning and sincerity of his request. I said, "You know, in the first place, those answers have to come from you. But perhaps the checkpoints in this book may provide you with the necessary insight to answer your own questions. As a matter of fact, I know you well enough to be certain that you are like a fine motor which may be sluggish at the moment but needs only a very elementary tune-up."

Over the past two years, I have been discussing the subject of individual achievement with men at all levels in business. At each meeting the following question was asked: "Assume that you were to mark yourself in your work on the scale of 0 to 10. At a zero level you would do nothing all day; at a 10 level, however, you would be functioning at the peak of your abilities. How would you score yourself on the scale of 0 to 10?" At this point, the same question was discussed in terms of activities outside of business (horizontal potential).

As a result of these questions, there emerged an achievement index, or a level of achievement, for each man. This began to take on increasing meaning and importance as I discovered that it usually related to a man's ability to fulfill himself and to extract the most enjoyment and happiness from his life.

It became apparent that every man in the group had etched into his mind a scorecard on which he is constantly marking and judging his own achievement index. No man took longer than a few seconds to score himself in these most complex areas of life. The marks ranged from 3 to 9. It was also apparent that each man was his own taskmaster and that his marks were like the ones he received in school. He either passed or flunked his own test. In other words, I found that if a man scored himself below a 7 in his work, he was most often not entirely happy with his level of performance and the negative impact on his life seemed to be considerable.

Similar conversations with other groups, however, also have led to the conclusion that as long as a man's composite achievement index is 7 or above (this would be the combination of his work rating and his rating of his home life, his cultural, recreational, and other pursuits), he felt reasonably good about himself, the direction of his life, and the use of his potentials. For example, one middle-management man put it this way: "I would score myself at a 5 level vertically. A good person will always have faster growth than the corporation can utilize. The large corporation becomes so structured that talents cannot be effectively utilized. You have to start doing other things. I find outlets in writing, teaching, and advanced seminars, for example, and this enables me to live with this 5 rating."

This book deals, however, with what the author believes is the primary problem, which is the need for a man to score himself at a 7 or better level in his chosen work. In other words, the principal thrust of a businessman's life centers around his sense of accomplishment in his work, with potential "spilling over" into his life outside of business.

Performance at a 4 or 5 level suggests a gap between

realized and unrealized potential, which can seriously affect a businessman's life. This gap can be illustrated in chart form. In looking at the drawing below, assume that a man has a capacity of 2 when he starts his chosen work. As the years progress, his potential grows through experience and training. In the third year, the dotted line assumes that his performance begins to level out at a 5, while his real potential curve continues on to what could be a 9 level.

A conversation with a very astute salesman tends to illustrate what a potential gap can mean. He said, "I think the knowledge that I can do more would have to frustrate anybody who has any sense, because I think there is a certain amount of waste when a person doesn't make use of his potential—waste of himself, of his family, and of social contribution in general. If I had an easy answer to this question, I probably would be using it. This is the big problem in business. You know, why doesn't everyone who is in this business do 25, 50, or 100 percent more work, assuming that they're not just lazy and have no desire at all? But we have to go out and create business. We all have different levels of ability. Some of us have abilities way up here, some in the middle, and some further down. The

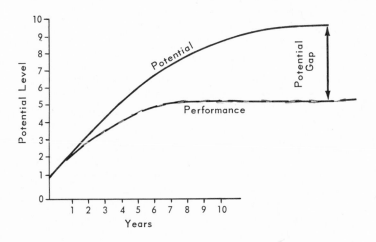

difference in ability is inherent among us and in the general nature of things. But whether your fundamental ability is at a high level or at a low level, if you're using only half of what it is, it's wasted."

On the other hand, consider this conversation with one of the most extraordinary men I have ever talked to. He scores himself at a 9 level vertically (only two men scored themselves at this level) and he said, "A guy has to constantly reassess goals so as to always be an achiever, and not alone in business. In this way he retains his vigor, his vitality. He needs at all times to be able to say, 'Hey, I'm achieving my goals.' He's got to enjoy his chosen field."

One other illustration at a 7 achievement: This young man, age 35, has an unusual situation in that he works in a senior capacity in his father's firm, so that the road was partially cleared for him in business. He said, "I score myself a 7. My reason is that to go higher I would have to bring work home at nights and on weekends, and travel much more. I'm not willing to pay this price. I want to spend this time with my family." I know for a fact that this man is very effective during his working hours, and that his potential is applied just as purposefully to other pursuits.

A vertical achievement level greater than 7 is very much an individual judgment, but the increasing complexity of business life makes a 4 or 5 level an untenable and often dangerous position. At a 4 or 5 level a man may be passed over in his job, be demoted, or even lose his job. Aside from these factors, the most serious effect often lies in needlessly not fulfilling oneself, in missing out on an important part of life. For example, a senior executive of a large industrial company sadly mentioned a middle-aged man who had been twice shuffled to other jobs in the company because his work had been going downhill. He said, "It's pathetic. He walks around the halls with his head down and never smiles. He's a beaten man. We won't fire him because he's been around too long."

Many illustrations will be used throughout this book of various achievement ratings that men apply to themselves. No one can say that any one mix of vertical and horizontal potential is correct for everybody. It is obvious that each man should do his own thing, subject to two caveats:

1. A personal rating below 7 in his chosen work is often inimical to his development if it persists. In any event, a minimum composite achievement of 7 is required for self-fulfillment.
2. Because potential, or the lack of it, tends to ramify, it may be difficult to develop horizontal potential to the point where it brings a low business achievement figure up to a satisfactory composite total. In other words, a low achiever in his work will tend to be a low achiever in his other activities.

In the context of this book, an individual who scores a 7 or above is an achiever. A level of 7, therefore, is not a mark that indicates a man is just getting by—he feels good about what he is doing. If he does not, he will ordinarily assign himself a lower rating. There is a marked relationship in a vertical score above 7 to the number of hours an achiever is spending at his work and in the development of his vertical competence. At a level of 9 an individual is fully committed to his work. He usually works sixty to seventy hours a week, and he enjoys it. A man at a level of 7 often seeks a broader base of activities which relate to his family and his recreational and cultural pursuits. He may work smarter, not harder. He is an achiever. The reasons for a vertical score below 7 are many—for example, not enough money, a lack of self-respect, boredom, resentment, or what may appear to him to be a lack of opportunity. The net result is frustration, which in itself inhibits potential and accentuates the problem. Those businessmen with a vertical score of 4 or 5 should find the checkpoints of potential especially interesting.

Growth

Over the past twenty-five years it has been fascinating and absorbing to observe friends rise to positions of great responsibility in corporations, and to see men reach exceptional levels of achievement nationally in the sales field. Certainly, one of the most fascinating studies of all time concerns the circumstances that motivate an individual to great achievement. Is it talent? Drive? Hours of work? Perseverance? Courage? Empathy? Faith? Belief? Or a combination of these and other factors?

Through the years the answer to these questions became of increasing interest, and I began a search that led through most of the current literature on the subject of success, spoke to groups that specialized in the behavior of man, and pursued other studies in the field of human behavior. A vital part of this consuming study lay in the personal observation of people as they struggled to grow and in the conversations with them about their growth. Those men who were growing did so without negative stress. They were aware of the challenge of growth, and seemed to be having the best time. It wasn't that they had an easy road; on the contrary, they worked unusually long hours. As one man said to me, "Don't think the road is easy. It's like the man said, 'Dying's easy, it's living that's hard.' But I'm so busy working with goals that are important to me, that I haven't time to worry about myself. And I have found that when I am interested, enthusiastic, and busy, I seem to get twice as much done with half the effort, and I enjoy myself."

The messages that began to emerge from this search related more and more to the capacity of each of us to develop more fully our own unique potential—our potential to enjoy life more fully, our potential to earn a greater income from our work, and our potential to develop latent talents. In addition to the message of potential, it became increasingly apparent that the realization of potential depends in a major way upon our ability to control our minds, and that the extent to which we can fulfill ourselves, or to realize ourselves, depends in a major way upon our capacity to discipline our minds on a structured basis. It also seemed clear that while there is much available information which relates to the mind and the structuring of the mind, this information is not coordinated or integrated in a usable form, and that there is a real need to synthesize and to coordinate the thought processes for developing potential.

The vast majority of books dealing with human behavior and achievement cover in one way or another the specific elements of how an individual climbed the ladder of success. Many describe merchandising techniques or how someone became an instant success. Others offer generalized descriptions of the principles of perseverance, persistence, discipline, enthusiasm, and all the other specific qualities that are important to an individual's success.

While specific qualities are of the utmost importance, it seems to me that the most important element in the development of a man's potential in his work and his life lies in his understanding of certain basic mental and physical processes that are conducive to success, and which need to be coordinated and used as a total process. But in no publication could I find a select list of habits that would fulfill every person; there were just too many differences between men in what they wanted out of life. Nevertheless, I began to discern an underlying structure of characteristics and life mode which seemed to be common to all the men I admired, one on which they had formed a firm foundation upon which they had built their success. Each had found the life he wanted and which was right for him. I call this structure "the process of realizing our own, unique, potential." It is a concept based on self-motivation, self-discipline, and conscious growth. It is not for the fainthearted.

In effect, the "process of realizing our potential" emerges as a way of life, as a code of behavior, which depends for its existence on an understanding of structured mental processes involving our thoughts, our attitudes, our feelings about ourselves and our work, and on our ability to love and to give freely of ourselves to others.

Potential

Human potential represents abilities and capacities which exist, but which are unused by, and often unknown to, an individual. In the broad sense, realizing one's potential involves experiencing life to its fullest, the ability to find joy in each day, and the realization that one is alive and that his lease on life is not indefinite. Specific potential exists in man's capacity to stimulate his creativity and productivity in his life and his work, and to develop and discover talents that he does not know exist. Great potential exists for improving our relationships with those around us and thus allowing us the opportunity to grow in return. There is potential for developing our concerns about our community and our environment.

Every individual has not only these potentials, but also the opportunity to remove self-imposed obstacles to realizing full potential. Self-imposed limitations may be more severe and restrictive than those imposed by a lack of physical or mental ability. For example, a negative attitude is an important limitation which can permeate every facet of a man's life.

This book deals with two classes of potential. First is the unused potential which becomes apparent when a man scores himself. For example, if he scores himself at a 7 level, he is obviously aware that a gap exists between what he is and what he can be. This gap may be of his own choosing or may occur because of personal or job difficulties which he has been unable to surmount. But he is aware that this potential exists, and he is able, if he wishes, to work on its development.

Second is the broad and important spectrum of individual potential that lies below the surface. This potential is not only dormant but is also unrecognized and can lie fallow for a lifetime. Grandma Moses is an example of undiscovered potential, for she was age 79 before she discovered her latent ability to paint, which had been unused most of her life. Becoming aware of unknown potential has great significance in enabling a man to develop new levels of competence and productivity in his work and in increased enjoyment of life. The four-minute mile, for example, was always a dream until Roger Bannister achieved it. At that point it immediately became a standard goal for all good runners. Awareness that potential exists is therefore the first step toward realizing it.

A New Self-Concept

There is a growing awareness of the value of these un-tapped individual resources, and a new self-concept is emerging as a result. The businessman is becoming increasingly aware of his uniqueness and of the fact that he has enormous reserves of untapped energy and potential which make up his total being. This self-concept involves a growing realization that as his potential begins to unfold, he becomes more integrated, more whole, and that a healing process occurs which can eliminate inner conflict.

The growth of this concept does not ordinarily involve rapid change, and one of the purposes of this book will be to indicate the long-range impact of the development of potential from the perspective of the businessman. The deeper his awareness of his own promise, the greater the opportunity to maximize productivity and growth, and the active use of his strengths and latent abilities can inject a quality of excitement and freshness into his daily experience. The techniques described in this book are designed to develop hidden resources and the creative ingenuity which enable a man to develop his own avenues of self-realization. This new self-concept recognizes that a man's past need not determine his future. The important value-judgment for him to make is what he is now and what he chooses to become. What he can be and what he will be depends on what he is willing to pay the price to be and what he is actively striving to become.

The message and the beauty of the realization of our potential for living was vividly illustrated in the case of Lewis Russell of Indianapolis, the world's longest-living heart transplant patient. When he celebrated the fifth anniversary of his surgery with an open house for friends, Russell said, "These have been the best years of my life." Mr. Russell, a teacher, for obvious reasons understood better than most the meaning of living, of growth, of self-renewal, of self-motivation. The phenomenal success of the book *Jonathan Livingston Seagull* is an outstanding reflection of the interest people have in the subject of potential. This is a story of growth, the unwillingness of a seagull to be confined within ordinary limits of a gull's life. Jonathan wanted to be free, to soar, to fly as no gull had flown before. He wanted to be alive, vital, and to seek to realize his potential for flight. The reason for the great interest in this story is obvious: No one wants to be an ordinary bird, for deep within us we all want to soar, we all want to explore our potential in life.

The process of realizing potential was developed to deal specifically with certain human tendencies which can easily prevent a man from soaring. These tendencies relate most often to the difficulty of self-motivation, which can cause a man to level off his objectives too quickly in his life and work, and often long before he has begun to realize his full potential. Unfortunately, unused, untested abilities tend to atrophy, just as unused muscles do. The less we use them, the more they become inert. This neglect of capability inhibits the full enjoyment of life. The process of realizing potential is a step-by-step guide to assist a man in preparing himself to grow, to serve, to motivate himself on a continuing basis.

The Process of Realizing Potential

The styles of those men who rate themselves high on the scale of potential reveal that, while the potential of each is unique, they seem to share a structured mental process which resists premature leveling of objectives and which uses a logical mind in a beneficial and helpful way. This process of realizing potential tends to be utilized by a minority of men because it involves a series of components which must be fully coordinated, and this fact is not simple nor well understood. This coordinated process is related to the development of the intellect and, very importantly, to the production of individual energy, for you may have observed that very successful people quite often possess a high level of energy.

For purposes of clarity, visualize a heating plant in a

building. As you know, such a system has a boiler into which fuel is fed which is then ignited. The heat energy produced is then distributed through ducts throughout the building. At the point of hot air delivery the cold air is returned to the boiler and the process repeats itself. The building superintendent determines the level of heat by controlling the thermostat.

From a conceptual viewpoint, the process of realizing our potential utilizes our own energy and intellect in a somewhat

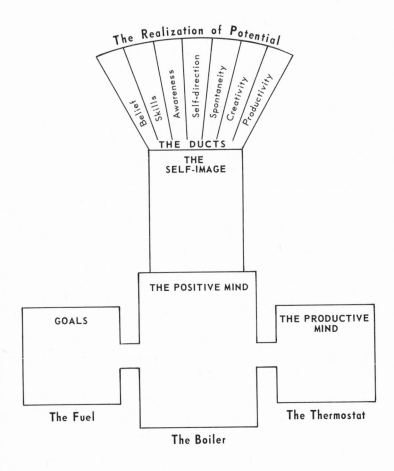

similar manner. The boiler is represented by our positive mind, which is the basis for the creation of our potential. The specific components of the positive mind are supported by a philosophy and desire for growth, and are represented by faith and belief in one's self, the enjoyment of one's work, and the ability to respond in a positive way to pressure or stress.

The fuel for the positive mind is our goals, which activate and give meaning to the positive mind. Exciting goals are a sure cure for boredom and frustration, for the energized mind automatically seeks to achieve them. When we combine exciting goals with dedication to our work, belief in ourselves, and with a positive response to pressure, we have the basic ingredients needed to eliminate a premature leveling-out process and to produce maximum energy.

The ducts that distribute the results and energy produced by positive mind and goal structuring stem from our own self-image, and this image is projected in an observable way through awareness, skills, belief, self-direction, spontaneity, creativity, and productivity. There is no judgment more important to our well-being than the image we create of ourselves, what we think we are now, and what we think we are capable of doing in the future.

The thermostat is the control we exercise in the structuring of our mental directives to determine productivity. For example, in goal setting, we can set lukewarm objectives, or we can deliberately intensify this process through the principles of goal structuring so as to develop a higher level of performance.

The ultimate object of this process is self-fulfillment through the development and blending of our mental, physical, and spiritual potentials.

The Search for Potential

The process of realizing potential is more than a concept. It is practical and workable, and is observable in the lives of successful people. There is nothing rigid in this process and a man can board the potential train at any one of a number of stations, but he is constantly engaged in a round trip which continues throughout life. For example, one man may begin his growth because of his love for his work, or another because of his interest in money, or another because he seeks recognition from other people. The important point is not why the search for potential begins. What is important is that the development of potential in a man's work becomes automatic so that it triggers development of potential in other areas of his life as well. In a sense, the process represents a chain which is only as strong as its weakest link; the highest level of energy and intellect is produced only when all of the components of the process are being utilized fully; when one component weakens, the level of energy—and therefore the man's output—is reduced.

An understanding of the factors in developing potential provides guideposts for growth and points up the fact that growth is, to an important degree, determinable by a man; that he can determine his course on the basis of a set of principles rather than let the events and tensions of the day control his life. This book provides these guideposts for the man who wants to soar, who wants to motivate himself, to fulfill himself, and who is willing to pay the price in terms of self-discipline to do so. The process outlined in these pages has a built-in strength due to its flexibility. It is not fixed like an algebraic equation. The term "potential" is an all-encompassing one and may mean different things to different people, but the various paths to its realization all arrive at the same goal. It follows that each person should choose a route to fit his own pattern. The relative importance of the components of potential may be debated in the order in which they are set forth, but their primary purpose is to enable an individual to construct his own map so that he can reach his destination at whatever the pace he chooses.

The process of realizing potential enables an individual to evaluate the need for coordination between the various components and their effect on one another. It also will enable him to get to the root of the reasons for a particular problem which may be hindering his growth. For example, a man may have to reexamine occasionally his desire to grow and the possibility that he is in fact leveling out, that is, getting stuck in a groove. If he finds that he is not growing, in spite of a desire to do so, it may be that his goals are lukewarm and are not properly structured. Or, a man may find that his self-image is being impaired because he is not approaching his job with a positive mind, so he may have to reappraise his entire range of feelings about his work. A man may also be inhibiting his rate of growth and impairing his self-image because he is overreacting to certain elements of his life, and is therefore inducing a negative response to pressure.

The specifics of each step in the process will be developed in this book on a step-by-step basis along with the many interrelationships between the components of the positive mind, goals, the self-image, and the structuring of the mind itself. The actual application of these steps is a highly personal matter because of the uniqueness of each person. For example, assume you were evaluating for an executive the factors involved in his work which pertain to his positive mind. You would be considering (1) his desire to realize his potential, (2) his faith and belief in himself and his work, and (3) his ability to respond to pressure. On a scale of 0 to 10, you might rate him a 9, based on his desire to do a fine job. Your rating of his faith in himself and his ability to respond to pressure might, however, be scaled at a level of 5, and you might finally rate his belief in his work at a level of 2, and that would be the cause of his problem. You find that he views the job negatively. Because of his feelings he responds poorly to pressure and to his own belief in himself. Because he does not view his job as a golden opportunity to serve people, to grow, and to earn an excellent income, he affects every step in the process of realizing his job potential. His goal structuring and his self-image most certainly have been impaired, and his potential gap has become so great that he has stopped at an inadequate level.

Because of the importance of one's major work in developing potential, this one factor—in this case a poor appraisal of his work—has far-reaching effects on this man. Once he understands this, however, he can either seek a work he can love or, more likely, change his mental approach to the job from negative to positive. At that point he begins to trigger the powerful responses which are available in the other steps in the process, and can in fact come to truly love his work because of the cumulative and coordinated effects of developing his potential.

Another approach to an evaluation of potential might be to consider the visible effects of a man's enthusiasm, demonstrated by an overtly expressed self-image. It may require careful evaluation to determine the reasons for a lack of enthusiasm and optimism. If it relates to the man's evaluation of himself, his self-image is unsatisfactory. In turn, this may occur because of a weakness in goal structuring, represented by an inability to clearly define and visualize worthwhile goals, and by the lack of incentive, a forcing system, to achieve goals. In the case of the older executive, the loss of enthusiasm can often be traced to a weakening in the basic desire to achieve his potential, which he sustained successfully for so many years.

It is interesting to appraise the job of an executive who has the task of getting his people to exercise their own responsibility for their own growth. How do you excite and interest the men under you, when each person is unique and needs to be treated differently? The head of a large advertising agency said to me recently that his creative people are the first to scream for money and at the same time are the first to say it is the least important to them. They are looking for stimulating, exciting goals and for recognition of their leadership.

The concept of the production of energy and intellect in terms of a process or system provides the basis for individuals and managers to begin to determine inefficiencies in that system and therefore in the production of potential.

The coordinated, sequential use of the factors for growth has a cumulative effect. It is an observable phenomenon that very outstanding individuals in the fields of music, art, medicine, and business have tremendous reserves of energy and that they often live unusually long and rewarding lives. Their capacity to enjoy life and their work has little relationship to money as they grow older; its foundation rests on their potential in their chosen field, which triggers the development of potential in all areas of their lives.

Men and women of this type are deeply involved in the process of realizing their own, unique potential. Their stress reactions are minimal; they love their work; they are strongly goal-oriented and understand the principles of goal structuring; they have a very satisfying self-image; and their minds have structured habits which make the process automatic. While they make their work look easy, it has developed because of dedication and integrity to the steps in the process of realization. They have a track to run on. While ordinary mortals are not as talented as those with special gifts, the opportunity to motivate one's self, to realize one's self, is a structured process which can be learned and taught.

The harmonious and coordinated blending of the components of the "process of realizing our potential" leads ultimately to the development of the mental, physical, and spiritual dimensions of potential, or what is sometimes called the "whole person." There are, however, certain tendencies that are difficult to resist and which prevent many men from realizing their potential.

The Leveling Process

The person who is truly self-motivated often rises very quickly to the top in his field, for he is an uncommon person who has both discipline and tenacity of purpose. It is very exciting to watch young people become outstanding in the sporting world. In addition to talent, they illustrate the unusual discipline and dedication that is necessary in their sport to win. We know that we are motivated by what is expected or demanded of us: For example, we have unexpected powers in times of crises. But we still do not know much about the remarkable differences in motivation which exist between one man and another. Why does one man fight on while another admits defeat? Or, why is one individual constantly renewing himself while another does not? It is known, however, that there is a marked tendency for a person to stop growing too soon in key areas of his life so that he then ceases to motivate himself.

Once a person finishes his formal education, he may increasingly limit the variety and scope of his life. This limitation of experience tends to increase as a person grows older. He often associates with a more limited number of people. His interests may narrow, and he settles more and more into a set pattern of doing things. He may lose the exhilaration he has experienced in his surroundings, and then cease to look with real interest at people's faces, or whatever else is going on for that matter. Unless some major change occurs—a new job, a move to a new city, marriage, a breakdown in his established habits—he may remain unaware of the limitations that he has subconsciously imposed on himself, and he does not take advantage of his resources and abilities, which he does not know exist.

But such a situation is difficult to correct because there is great resistance to change. Once a man's pattern of life has fallen into a groove, the admonition "know thyself" may be discarded and the process of reappraising strengths and weaknesses is forgotten. There are many people who, even if they are aware that they have unused potential, do not want to change even if they know they could. Their answer is, "So what! I make enough money for my needs, I enjoy my television and my family and friends, and that's enough for me." But there are increasing numbers of people who want to grow, who don't want to settle for less than what should be theirs *now;* who don't want to retire and find life a complete bore; who don't want to have to say someday, "Why do we just start to live and then have to die?" And there are creative men in business who want to grow, but who can't put it all together.

Consider the normal development of a businessman. He is hired by his company after most extensive testing and interviewing. He may then embark on a training program designed to equip him to properly do his job, and he operates under close management supervision. Because of the difficulties of learning and his newness in his job, he applies himself enthusiastically and with great effort so that he can begin to produce the results expected of him. After some time he becomes mature, his skills increase, and the supervision of management begins to lessen. At some point during these early years a leveling-off process often begins to occur. Slowly, imperceptibly, the furnace is banked; slowly, imperceptibly, the man turns down his termostat. As his money needs are increasingly satisfied, he may unconsciously begin to attempt to perpetuate his present situation. This is where the problems start, for the truth is that life is a journey, not a destination, and a person can go downhill faster than he went up.

It used to be that a young man climbed the ladder of success. In today's complex economy that ladder is more like a greasy pole. In the normal course of events, when the leveling process begins, the creative man begins to feel his first tinge of boredom, and his job may become repetitious. He begins to slow down and his enthusiasm lags. He may then begin to develop certain substitutes for the use of his potential. Given a group of men who are of apparently equal ability and education, we observe that their training and results are not usually much different in their early years. As time passes, one man will begin to stand out, and then another, while the productive results of others will climb slowly and many will begin to level out, to settle into a groove.

A man who desires to move toward his potential must take into account the natural tendency to level out. The real problem, however, is in leveling out too soon, where the gap between performance and potential becomes too great. For example, a man may be temporarily blocked in his job by lack of a skill or because of someone who is senior to him in position, and he finds his progress impeded. He may try and try again to surmount the problem, but if he quits he may permanently be grooved into his existing performance level, which can be far below his real potential. Or a man may, as his financial needs are reasonably met, decrease his work output as his skills increase so as to wind up with the same result with a continuing decrease in effort. Leveling out prematurely is an extreme handicap to further growth and the use of potential, for it is very difficult to change an established pattern of life once it becomes firmly fixed prematurely.

There are many versions of the leveling process. For instance, in a group of executives in their fifties, it was agreed by most of them that although they had highly paid, responsible jobs, they had really lost a great deal of interest in their work. They were, in effect, bored. This seems to be a fairly common complaint among men in this age group because, while their abilities remain unimpaired and their capacity for service has not diminished, there is often a lessening of their interest and enthusiasm in what they are doing. Unless they consciously begin to explore and to reexplore their potential, there can be a definite and undesirable effect on their work and their lives.

The inclination toward leveling out often relates to the belief that we can maintain the status quo in life, when in reality everything we do or have is in a state of flux and continued change. It is hard to believe that in recent years we have had the collapse of the Penn Central Railroad, that a President of the United States has resigned, and that the automobile industry has been thrown into a chaotic situation because of the energy crisis. An executive with a large corporation stated recently that for many years he sat in executive sessions with a group of a dozen men and that these men seemed stolid and immutable; that, in effect, because they had always been there, they would always be there. Now, after a period of a relatively few years, he looks around the room and observes that half of these men are no longer there; they have either retired or they have died.

A friend recently remarked that life is an inclined plane and, as a practical matter, the concept of leveling or of considerable nonuse of potential, particularly as applied to large segments of a person's life, is destructive to the human organism. The fact is that the tendency to level out at any stage in life must be resisted for our own best interests. We either go forward or backward in life. We face the natural tendency to constrict our growth as we get older, as well as the fact that the less of our potential that we use, the more this tendency increases.

Horizontal or Vertical Growth?

One of the pressing questions most men in business face at some point in their career is whether or not to stay with their present job. Men often get locked into a particular job and may be unable, at a given time, to change that fact. For example, there may be two vice-presidents ahead of a man, age 45, who are about his age; unless something unforeseen happens, our man knows that his vertical progress with his company is probably blocked until he retires. He has several choices:

1. If he is a risk taker, he may seek opportunity elsewhere which uses and pays for his potential. The capacity to take risks is very often the difference between mediocrity and success in business.

2. He may resign himself to his fate and begin a destructive leveling-out process.

3. He may pursue the job he has with dedication born of service, but he may also develop his potential horizontally. He may broaden his outside interests to include community pursuits, or painting, or other recreational areas of his life. Life for this man can be rewarding because he continues to grow. He does, however, maintain a minimum achievement index of 7 in his work.

The majority of people will never be vice-presidents of a company; indeed, they may not want to be. But they can find life enormously satisfying. A middle-management man, age

45, said to me, "I score myself an 8½ in my business and an 8 in my other activities. I have no great worlds to conquer. I love my work and find it challenging. I think you have to like yourself."

On the other hand, a well-known psychologist said recently, "I'd say 75 percent of corporation employees, including a lot of presidents and vice-presidents, are very anxious, fearful people by nature and fundamentally insecure. Much of the internal conflict grows out of people's reactions to what they perceive as threats to their security. Most stay with one company, not out of loyalty but because they lack the courage to quit and try something new. One of the biggest problems is the incapacity of many executives to tolerate strong subordinates. I can't tell you the number of companies I've seen composed of cringing wretches." Even if this statement is watered down, it is not a pretty picture.

Realistically, a man in the business world faces some hard decisions in the course of his working lifetime. A man must learn to live with the power structure and the politics of a corporation, and he most certainly has to watch the maneuvering for position that goes on around him. A man must also evaluate his potential for progress within a company and perhaps at some point take risks in order to achieve potential with another organization. There are no easy answers to this problem, but perhaps a man can best deal with the complexities of the business world if he is in a continuous process of realizing his own potential. Instead of structuring his business life around office politics, wheeling and dealing to seek personal gain, and living in fear of younger talent, he looks to his own growth, supported by a philosophy of giving, for his sustenance. In this way he can develop the inner strength and reserves of courage, faith, love, and enthusiasm which can carry him over the rough spots.

The development of potential, both horizontally and vertically, increasingly puts a man in charge of himself. Through the disciplines of growth he tends to free himself of self-destructive habits.

Substitutes for Potential

The decision not to level out in business or personal life is vital to the individual. There is also a constant search under way by corporations in which the basic question is asked, "How can we develop the full potential of our men?" Consider the importance of human potential in terms of the question, "How can we motivate our men to do a better job?" This question is predicated on the fact that the ability of the executive and sales arm of the company to produce the product and to move the merchandise determines ultimately the profitability of the company. It is small wonder, therefore, that the growth of the individual is of such great concern to all members of the corporation.

It is fascinating to observe large groups of businessmen at work. It is my experience that of a hundred men, ten will excel on average; and of those ten individuals, two will particularly stand out. The earnings of men who are in the same business environment can vary enormously. Corporations try to provide every possible incentive to develop potential among their men who exhibit the desire to grow. There are stock option programs, bonuses, deferred compensation, awards, and recognition for achievement. In short, no stone is left unturned to motivate the individual, but the one which is the most critical of all—the ability of the individual to continuously realize his own potential and to avoid leveling out—depends on his own ability to directly motivate himself. If a creative man ceases to be motivated by money or other incentives, and therefore attempts to perpetuate an existing situation, he can begin to create substitutes for the use of his potential, which can be harmful to his development.

Where the gap between actual performance and potential becomes too great, substitutes are often freely used to protect the individual's ego, his self-esteem. For example, a man's excessive use of alcohol to cope with the frustration of his work may indicate a retreat from reality, an escape mechanism to avoid the hard facts of a job. In essence, substitutes for potential are closely related to the leveling-out process, which in turn is often related to a man's frustration, occurring perhaps because of a temporary inability to advance further and more quickly in his work, or in the nonuse of other potentials. There may also be a certain security enhanced by substitutes, and while frustration may be painful, people learn to live with this pain and to become comfortable with it. The premature leveling process that occurs can become habitual, and men will strongly resist any attempt by someone else to alter what becomes a "comfort zone."

On the surface, most people do not show frustration, but under circumstances of extreme confidence a person may confess that he is not entirely happy with his life and wishes it could be different. Substitutes for lack of opportunity to use potential can affect a person both emotionally and physically, while also limiting a person's ability in his work. Thoreau said, "Most men lead lives of quiet desperation," and our affluence has probably not altered the validity of this statement.

There are many examples of substitutes for potential which are used by those who do not work for money. For the person who does not have the discipline of a paying job and a boss, it is often easier under these circumstances to allow the gap between performance and potential to become too great. For example, a man who retires may have this problem, and he can go through a very trying period because of the need to start from scratch in finding his new potentials. Consider the following business substitutes for potential which are quite common.

"I've Got It Made"

In this case a man has had steady successes and perhaps in the past year or two has been unusually successful. He begins to awaken to the fact that life is indeed good and that his accomplishments are very clear. He is respected by his company or his friends. While he basks in this success, he sits back and says to himself, "I've got it made." At that moment he is setting the stage for trouble. His satisfaction implies that he has reached a plateau where he can maintain his standing without struggle. There is an expression used by men in their own business which best describes this thought process, "A hero one year, a bum the next." The "I've Got It Made" syndrome denotes a slowdown of basic winning processes. In contrast, a professional operates free of tension, and never slows his forward motion or his momentum except for planned relaxation periods.

"The Marketplace Is Saturated"

In this case a mature man may begin to conclude that, because of increasing competition and the development of the competition in his particular field, more and more of his products or services have been taken over by other professionals. He mistakenly thinks there is a shrinking market for what he produces. While it is a very real fact that the products and skills of others are constantly improving, and while the difficulty of getting new business can increase because of competition, the demand for products and services is also increasing at such a rate as to make our individual skills more important. Therefore, the "Marketplace Is Saturated" concept is really fallacious and points up the fact that continued growth is absolutely essential in today's world.

"Let Management Do It"

When the businessman deserts his adult status and reacts rather than acts, he may become increasingly dependent on other members of the management team and assume a role which resembles that of a child for his parents. Instead of operating maturely and depending on himself for results, he tends to look to others to provide him with support, and he is very apt to blame his troubles on others. He often believes it is up to others on the team to inspire him to do those things he does not like to do, and he can become irritated at what he believes are the weaknesses of the members of the team. This substitute leads to weakness and to negative thinking on the individual's part.

"Mañana"

Anyone at any stage of life can easily learn to use this substitute. In fact, this problem afflicts people at all levels. The shuffling and reshuffling of papers to defer action until tomorrow is a trap even the most alert individuals can fall into. The "mañana" substitute is particularly insidious for three reasons: It tends to stifle creative thinking; the accumulation of detail prevents the man from focusing on those elements of a job which require intense concentration; and the human mind does not take kindly to the unnecessary accumulation of detail. It has been said that "work expands to fill a vacuum," and the needless deferral of action until tomorrow accentuates this tendency.

"I've Got to Get Organized"

It is surprising how many men feel the need to get organized. The inability to properly and systematically organize one's work seriously impedes the full use of potential. The basic symptom of this substitute is expressed by a person who never seems to be able to get all the pieces together at one time and does not relate to his daily activities. There can be a wide variety of causes for a man's inability to get organized, but very often this problem will occur when an individual has leveled out somewhat and when he is practicing the mañana technique. The "I've Got to Get Organized" syndrome can gradually substitute permanently for the use of potential.

"Last Man Out"

This is a comfort substitute for the use of potential. It develops when a business matures and develops a substantial clientele of customers. There is a very natural tendency to work with people we know, and who know us, and to constantly rework friendly markets. When this substitute is used, the individual or the company can gradually lose skills in the creation of new markets so that, imperceptibly, the circle of old customers becomes smaller and smaller. Thus, over the years, clientele would be constantly lost until eventually there would remain only one customer. When that customer died, the businessman or the business would have successfully joined the "Last Man Out" club. This illustrates a very human tendency to work within an individual's "comfort zone," an area in which creative people can operate relatively free of tension. This is also true of most of the substitutes used for potential. Unfortunately, this type of comfort zone is not very productive and will result eventually in financial penalties.

Mediocrity

Mediocrity is a characteristic which is often accepted as a norm. A senior executive with a large company said to me recently, "We don't want too many aggressive people. We have too few top jobs and we want people who will perform OK and who are content at a lower level." While the old saw that you can't have all chiefs and no Indians is valid, this approach is basically negative in character—somewhat like viewing a half-glass of water as half empty rather than half full. It tends to foster mediocre performance as a way of life. A man may easily adjust to mediocrity if it is someone else's standard. He does his expected job, but does not extend himself. His experiences are repetitive rather than cumulative. His chief concern is in perpetuating an existing situation, and he ceases to grow. He may have the capacity to grow, but he loses his potential for growth. Although the use of potential should be fostered by business management, in the final analysis it must come from within the individual. Its foundation is certainly not conformity, rigidity, or a restricted philosophy.

Mediocrity may be considered the stagnation of competence well below a man's abilities. In a sense, this means that a man settles for second best. His motto is apparently "don't rock the boat," or "don't make waves," and his primary interest is often security and the least amount of tension in his work.

Yet, in my study I found that those who scored themselves low in terms of their own special achievement were not truly fulfilled. Their question was often, "What do I do next?" From a practical standpoint some felt that they were at an impasse in their jobs, or that they had a boss who didn't inspire them, or that their work had problems they couldn't solve. Such analyses, real or imaginary, curb potential, for the truth is that every man wants to feel that he can do something better than anyone else. Men have pride, and intuitively they don't want to be second best.

The solution to the problem is elusive because many of us instinctively look to others to motivate us. The avoidance of mediocrity in terms of our own individual potential means that we begin to move in a new direction. Our goals are not only extrinsic in terms of money, recognition, etc., but intrinsic in terms of our inner worth. Every person has an inherent desire to grow and to control his own destiny. It can sometimes involve one of the most difficult questions a man must face: "Which do I value most—my self-respect, my dignity, or my pension and group insurance plan?"

The process of realizing potential does not recognize either mediocrity or the compulsive pursuit of perfection as a basis for a satisfactory life-style. Its foundation is a goal-oriented, positive individual who is always growing vertically and horizontally, within the limits of his own particular competence.

The Desire for Growth

The person who is perfectly content with his life will, of course, have little desire to grow. But, suppose that an individual says to himself: "I recognize that the less of my potential

I use, the more constricted my approach to life will be. I want to avoid leveling out at any stage of my life and I want to grow and fulfill myself."

The man who sincerely says "I want to grow" has crossed the major barrier to growth itself. Without the thought, the goal, nothing will happen, and a man will continue along the same road throughout his life. In itself, a desire to grow implants a goal into the mind, and the mind will seek the methods to achieve that goal because an idea held strongly enough and long enough in the human mind will tend to become reality.

To illustrate some of the factors involved in growth, it is interesting to look at the motivation of a creative businessman. A vital question facing a corporation or an individual is this: How do you motivate a person to want to grow? or How does a man motivate himself to desire growth? Like a golfer, an individual establishes a business handicap, the scratch player being the superior performer and the 20-handicapper being a more modest performer. Early in his career a man will tend to establish or stabilize his handicap, and this is why it is so important to keep new men on a growth curve before they have time to settle prematurely into a high-handicap groove. The ultimate corporate and individual objective must be to enable the individual to establish the lowest handicap he can manage within the limit of his abilities, for the realization of human potential is a most desirable objective.

The realization of growth, however, can sometimes be a formidable task. For example, a person may think negatively; then one day he reads a book about positive thinking. The benefits are so obvious that the individual decides then and there that he will change his habits and begin to think positively. He may find, however, that after a period of time the new frame of mind wears off and his old negative manner of thinking returns. In other words, his old thought process is so strongly entrenched that as soon as incentive begins to fade, his mind reverts and again he is subjected to fear, tension, or worry. In the same way, the creative businessman has developed habitual thought patterns which come on strong and which are deeply ingrained in his mind. A man may periodically have the desire to change, but may lack the technique and discipline necessary to effect permanent change to a higher level of performance. Temporarily, a change for the better may be forced by a decrease in work results, but when the problem is solved, he resorts to substitutes.

External Motivators for Growth

In the business world there are several external factors which motivate men. For example, the creative person has chosen his work partly as a means of supporting himself and his family, and he often can—if he applies himself—reach a substantial income in a rather short period of time. However, as income continues to rise, motivation to grow for money reasons can diminish and, although this is a strictly individual matter, there is a point on the income scale where money loses its power to motivate men. The desire for money strongly motivates the newer man to reach higher and higher goals because of economic necessity; he is hungry and his results can reflect this fact. He is the "comer" in an organization and his interest and enthusiasm are an inspiration to those around him. As he matures and becomes successful and meets his money needs, he becomes the typical target for leveling out. Except for those few individuals who are truly money-oriented, an individual cannot count on money by itself for long-range motivation.

In addition to money, there is the human need for recognition, for "stroking," which begins at birth and never ceases during life. Organizations recognize this fact by providing executive offices, awards, money, and other perquisites, and the more outstanding the record, the greater the recognition. Recognition is an important factor in the growth of a man if he will permit it to be, but it, too, cannot necessarily be depended upon for continuous long-term motivation of men, for the reason that this type of recognition can lose meaning to many men, once they reach a certain economic level in life.

The third external motivator for the businessman is his boss, and it has been said with considerable truth that "the best fertilizer is the footprint of the boss." However, the job of inspiring and motivating men to realize their potential is a most difficult matter, for the principles of self-motivation are not well understood and may not be communicated or taught to others in a form which is practical and useful. The ability of a man to motivate others depends not only on his own personal understanding of the principles of motivation, but also on his actual ability to motivate himself.

To inspire a man to continue to grow toward his potential and to avoid the premature leveling process requires something more than money, recognition, and a boss. That something is, in part, a commitment and a decision on the part of a man to begin to grow and to discard those thoughts, attitudes, and habits which may have inhibited his growth.

The commitment to grow and realize potential can be inspired by the fact that a person has, figuratively, beaten his head against the wall in his business or personal life. He simply decides he has had enough. He may be unhappy, confused, and at the bottom of the barrel mentally. In short, he may be miserable enough to look for change. There are also those whose lives have become so boring, so uneventful, that they begin to question what it's all about, and they become desperate enough to want to seek change. Illness or some other traumatic event can interrupt the flow of an individual's life to the point where he also begins to question and reexamine his life.

The best reason for desiring growth, however, is that the process of realizing potential can be structured so that a man can see it in its whole perspective. The goal is to become a winner in one's work as well as in life outside of work, and to have fun doing it. The winner seeks to know himself and to be himself; he seeks to determine more fully his own destiny and to throw off thought patterns which are not only irrelevant but also inappropriate to his current living style. He rejects substitutes if they are harmful to him and to his growth; he rejects using his energies to maintain pretense and to manipulate other people for his selfish purposes. He rejects the role of a loser, whose work seems endlessly repetitious and who in effect has retired early, but still goes to work every day, puts in his time and makes a living, and waits for the success which never comes.

The man who decides adamantly that he wants to grow also determines to use more of his mind. The person who grows uses more of his mind than most other people; this is a major reason for his success. He does not have a more brilliant mind than others; he simply uses more of what he has. The individual who wants to develop potential avails himself of every possible technique to expand the more subtle areas of his mind. He renews himself through his ability to motivate and discipline himself, and this is the device by which boy wonders become men-leaders-creators-thinkers.

Self-Motivation

It is apparent that the relatively small percentage of men who truly motivate themselves, regardless of external circumstances, understand intuitively the need to grow, to continuously realize their potential, and are aware of the dangers of leveling out prematurely. Perhaps their sensitivity in these areas is due to guidance by their parents, or to influence of their business environment, or to their exposure to a great teacher, or to a natural competitive streak. But, for the larger percentage of men, the following principles of self-motivation become essential guidelines.

The need and desirability of a man's dedicating his life to the realization of his many potentials is vital to the development of self-motivation. In other words, it is urgent that a man, for his own best interest, deliberately avoid the premature leveling process, no matter what his age or his position in life.

The second factor that emerges as critical to the development of a person's self-motivation, of realizing his potential, is the need to become the master of his mind instead of its slave —in controlling his mind, with the basic purpose of having his mind take orders and not give them.

Self-motivation involves the recognition that the mind is like a machine or computer which processes the data fed into it. It is constantly seeking to solve the problems faced in reaching our goals, our objectives in our work, and our leisure life. For example, our minds are constantly feeding us facts as to whether or not we have sufficient money to do a certain thing, or how our businesses should be run, or what we should do with our leisure time. The mental machine is constantly in motion and is engaged in meeting crises and in dealing with moods of excitement, of depression, of frustration, and victories. If the mind is not controlled, it is not difficult to spend a good part of the day thinking about what may happen or what has happened, and we begin to lose the essence of what is happening right now. We spend our time thinking about living, but not in actual living.

The well-ordered mind operates much like the human digestive process. Once we take food into our mouths and swallow it, the digestive process becomes totally automatic. Our system digests the food and extracts from it the nutrients needed to sustain life. In the same way, the thoughts that we put into our minds are being absorbed by the brain and at that time the entire matter becomes mechanical and beyond control. The point is that unless our thoughts, as in the case with the food we eat, contain the proper nutrients, the mind will run out of control.

In a sense, our minds function like a powerful automobile. The automobile will move the driver to whatever destination he chooses and at whatever speed he selects, depending upon the amount of fuel he feeds to it. A vital part of living up to our potential lies in our capacity to structure the machinelike character of the mind in such a way that it directs us to our desired destination as well as controls the speed we use.

The impact of desire and motivation was commented on

recently by an outstanding professional golf instructor, Bob Toski. He said, "I think the thing we're going to have to find out about all these young players is how much of a price they are willing to pay to become great. You can't ever let your determination fade away. For example, Nicklaus was home for a couple of weeks earlier this year and wasn't planning to play for awhile. Suddenly, he tells his wife he's going back out. She can't very well tell him they need him at home. He's got to control his own destiny and she must encourage him. So Nicklaus got the urge and he showed up in Hawaii and won the tournament. The man still has great desire and determination. That's what makes Jack the player he is and that's what these young players must have if they are ever to come close to his record."

Summary

The process of realizing potential can prepare you to serve society, to maximize your income, and to enjoy every aspect in all areas of your life.

The rewards that come when a man motivates himself to grow occur largely within him—the qualities of independence, self-respect, and personal satisfaction. He controls himself and his destiny, and he is guided by his desire to achieve his own growth and potential to serve. He has a reason for living, for being, and his aliveness and awareness are recognized by all around him. John Ruskin put it in these words, "That man is richest who, having perfected the functions of his own life to the utmost, has also the widest, helpful influence."

The first of the major checkpoints on the path to realizing your potential is a positive mind. This would appear to be so elementary today that it might be assumed that reading the book *The Power of Positive Thinking* would forever end any further discussion of it. But, as a practical matter, a positive approach is so vital to growth that it must be constantly re-newed, and many careers falter on it. In terms of the golf swing, the positive mind is that which occurs before the club head is moved back slowly. It's the stance, the self-confidence, and the controlled relaxation that the golfer sets up in the "waggle" before he begins to swing. He programs his mind in a positive and automatic way for each swing. Even though he has performed the act perfectly thousands of times, he still needs to be reminded of the fundamentals.

As with the golf swing, each checkpoint in the process of potential is a part of the whole. The positive mind is activated by goals (the back swing), which in turn are reflected in our self-image (the club head at impact and the follow-through stroke). Through mind structuring we can begin to adjust the level of development of our own particular energy and intellect. How badly do we want to win and in what?

Our potential to live fully, to love and be loved, and to be successful in our chosen work depends on the fundamentals of a process that can be broken down into individual parts, but which function together in a free-flowing swing. This book looks first to the fundamentals and then to the totality of potential. In the ultimate sense, the swing of your life depends on the coordination of all its parts so that they strengthen each other.

2

Checkpoint 1 —
the positive mind

The process of realizing potential requires a positive approach to life as the foundation in building both intellect and energy. Have you noticed how you enjoy being around people who think positively and who seem to have a quiet purpose to their lives? You may have noticed that people who are negative can actually draw energy from you and leave you limp and exhausted after a session with them. The positive mind is an attitude, an approach to life, and is of such unparalled importance to our physical and mental well-being that one cannot pay too great a price to achieve it. It is a state of mind which can bring to its owner the positive emotions of optimism, courage, enthusiasm, and faith, as well as the release of stress. It has an enormous influence on one's vertical competence and on the enjoyment of life.

While a businessman has the potential to think positively, his capacity to do so is being tested every day. He is subjected in business to a wide range of pressures. For example, the younger man can often feel hemmed in by what he feels is a lack of opportunity and not enough money. One young banker said to me, "I rate myself vertically at about a 4 level. I admit I'm frustrated, but in these staid institutions I guess a man has to be patient." A change in business conditions can also have a marked effect on a man's outlook. The point is that when things are going well, when business is good, being positive is easy. The trick is to stay positive when things turn

41

sour. Moreover, as a person grows older, staying positive can be affected by sheer boredom, a change in management, or the challenge of strong young subordinates.

A person is also exposed to an avalanche of negative news relating to his business, the overall economic state of affairs, and the world in general. The point is that every businessman at every level is subject to these forces at varying times during his career.

Yet a positive state of mind is the foundation of both achievement and well-being! How, then, does one survive the input of crises and bad news? If things turn bad in spite of his best efforts, how does one stay positive? How does one rise from defeat and move on toward success? While this book presents no easy answers to these questions, it is suggested that a positive state of mind is a result of the use of what this writer calls "components" of realizing potential. These components involve self-understanding, self-motivation, and a desire to use our own potentials, with the ultimate goal being self-realization and self-fulfillment.

Each component is explained in this and succeeding chapters, and specific suggestions are offered for the development of each. Yet, a positive-thought process is but one segment of a much larger picture and is far more than merely the specifics of thinking the best or visualizing the best. Each component is, in fact, a part of a fluid ongoing process which functions when the going gets rough.

The positive mind, conceptually pictured as the boiler room, has three major attributes. First is the idea of a strong purpose and meaning to one's life; second, faith and belief in one's self and in one's major work; and third, a positive response to the pressures of life.

Component 1 — Purpose and Meaning of Your Life

A desire to grow, to move in the direction of realizing one's own potential, is basic to the positive mind. This would appear to be a perfectly obvious fact, but the truth is that many people are unaware of it and their lack of the desire to grow is the cause of much human misery.

The tendency to accept a status quo is a natural one and often occurs because of a very human desire to achieve a fixed state in life where an individual feels that he has solved his problems, or where he has constructed a stable and—what may appear to him to be—permanent world. The fact is that we are always in a state of fluidity, of constant change, and we can accept with certainty that in the long run we will either continue to grow and to realize our various potentialities, or we will begin the process of decline. The unexpected nature of change is illustrated by the case of an executive in a large company in Philadelphia, where he had worked approximately eighteen years. He had assumed, as most of us would, that he had a lifetime job. Suddenly the news broke that his division was being sold, and he found that what he had assumed was permanent had become uncertain.

It is interesting to ask people what their major purpose in life is. They will often look puzzled, for it seems that most of us do not take the time to reflect very often about this basic question. A famous concert conductor said recently, "I like to work with younger musicians because as men get older they cease to listen to the music. They are too busy playing and listening to themselves." Most of the answers about purpose in life seem to indicate that we are frequently sounding off in our own music and do not hear what life and the experience of the ages is trying to tell us. Yet, the ability of an individual to find a fundamental purpose and meaning to his life is essential to self-fulfillment. Man hungers to find the meaning of his life. Prior generations were more easily able to find this meaning in terms of religious experience and the relatively small world within which they lived. Amid the many complexities of this modern age, the search for meaning has become more difficult, and a person can find that what he thought was his purpose is in reality a limited goal which is rapidly submerged in the larger stream of everyday contingencies.

For example, it has become increasingly popular to assume that individual happiness comes when one achieves one's goals, and often these goals are centered on the acquisition of possessions, status or power, and—in its ultimate form—a life of ease in which a person can find true happiness. A typical picture is one of a man spending his days fishing on a beautiful lake or finishing his life on a golf course. While these activities are a part of the dream, the real story for the businessman also involves building toward meaningful goals, with the effort to achieve those goals requiring considerable use of one's powers and talents. This concept of striving in no way underrates the desirability of enjoying the pleasant way of life. Certainly it is everyone's right to enjoy the pleasures and the comforts which are available today through modern technology, and there is much to enjoy. The point, however, is that the enjoyment of the pleasant things of life is not enough, and this is borne out by the fact that we have large numbers of people in this country who are able to do and spend as much as they please on themselves and their pleasures, but who obviously don't exhibit any unusual degree of serenity and bliss.

In the context of this book, a person's purpose, meaning, and commitment to life are inseparable. The man with a strong purpose builds meaning into his system, and because of this he commits himself to his cause. A strong purpose can provide a foundation, the undergirding, for his life. There is nothing more exciting than to watch a man pursue an activity, for example, where he is strongly motivated. He is hungry for success. In the business world, strong motivation is often an attribute of the younger man, but the man who can continue to motivate himself as he grows older is more often the exception than the rule. There is a great need for a motivating and practical purpose in life which can be clearly understood. It should be a purpose strong enough to guide an individual in his working and personal activities and it should in effect provide a frame of reference for his life.

Defining your purpose can begin to provide the answer to some of life's basic questions: "What must I live up to?" "What are my obligations?" "To what must I commit myself?" "What will my goals be?" "How can I get the greatest satisfaction out of my life?" Individual answers to these questions cannot serve as a universal formula for everyone's commitments or goals because people will differ in their goals and in their life-style, in their thought processes, in their convictions, and in their natural talents. Yet, whatever you define as your purpose should be sufficiently worthwhile and valuable so that it may act as a foundation for your way of life.

The purpose suggested here as being the cornerstone of maturity is this: That an individual dedicate himself to the realization of his own unique potential for living fully. The starting point for self-fulfillment and self-realization must be an idea of power and exceptional vitality, that is, individual growth and the desire of a person to achieve his potential. This ideal should permeate all strata of his life and every one of his thought processes. It is a deep-seated desire to be in control of our lives and to be moving toward the ultimate development of what we can be. It is also a concept entirely inconsistent with the attrition of growth as we grow older.

The Purpose of Growth

Eleanor Roosevelt once said, "The purpose of life, after all, is to live it, to taste experience to the utmost, to reach out eagerly and without fear for newer and richer experiences." This contrasts vividly with the concept of a life based almost entirely on external goals and success defined primarily in terms of money and physical possessions. Yet this latter concept is as American as apple pie, and has made this country economically great. In effect, the counsel given by American parents to their children has been to get a good education, get a good job, get married, make all the money you can, and you will be happy. It implies that happiness is dependent solely on external circumstances and that when we consolidate our material position in life we have arrived. This concept is a myth.

Is the rather idealistic view of Mrs. Roosevelt that our

purpose is to live, to reach out for and taste richer experiences inconsistent with the competitive drive to earn and accumulate money so as to provide security for ourselves and our families? Will we begin to limit individual initiative, opportunity, and freedom because our concept of economic growth becomes inconsistent with a growing desire for personal fulfillment? Hopefully the answer will be no. The purpose of growth and the development of a man's own potential make these two viewpoints entirely compatible. The decision for the businessman becomes one of how much emphasis to place on his vertical as opposed to his horizontal potential. It does not in any way limit a desire to earn money but rather encourages the acquisition of money and external achievements. It also promotes internal growth based on one's own self-respect and sense of inner worth. The purpose of growth, therefore, is both intrinsic and extrinsic in its origins and motivations.

From a practical business viewpoint, the most important thing about realizing potential is that the strength which can hold a man to his purpose is not necessarily blind stubbornness but the real desire to grow. Bear in mind that success is achieved only by a minority of men and is therefore not a natural evolvement. It is ordinarily not achieved by following our natural preferences and prejudices, unless we are in the play area of our life. There are untold numbers of things men don't like to do. In business, they may not really like their jobs, or may not like to track their goals or to stay organized. At home they may not expand their minds by reading or by intellectual discussion, or by refraining from too much television, or food, or alcohol, or whatever. While everyone can list many things they don't like to do, the winner disciplines himself to do what he does not like to do so that he can accomplish the things he wants to accomplish. The man who has leveled out prematurely accepts methods of doing things which are pleasing to him; the winner seeks pleasing results. But most of all, the winner's purpose and the goals supporting it are clear enough and worthy enough to make him form habits of doing things he does not like to do if those things help accomplish his purpose. The man who wants to grow, who wants to serve, and who is goal-oriented has the leverage to bring him considerable business success.

A commitment to realizing potential in any phase of life is sufficiently compelling to commence the process of growth in that area. The person who can devote himself to a higher purpose finds himself. The great artist transcends himself, he loses himself, as he paints a master canvas. In much the same way the ultimate meaning in the purpose of realizing potential lies in giving our love through helping others. This assumes that the ultimate happiness in life is found in receiving love and affection, which we realize by increasing our ability to give accordingly, and this can come only from growth through introspection and discipline. We transcend ourselves when the big drive toward our fulfillment lies in the love of our fellowmen and not alone in our own selfish interests. What job, for example, does not offer this opportunity?

The Practical Implications of a Strong Sense of Purpose

Robert F. Kennedy once said, "Each time a man stands up for an ideal, or acts to improve the lot of others . . . he sends forth a tiny ripple of hope . . . these ripples build a current that can sweep down the mightiest walls of oppression and resistance." The ideal of realizing one's own potential has a cumulative effect. For example, a strong purpose provides self-motivation on a consistent and continuing basis. Self-motivation, or the ability of an individual to energize himself, is one of the most vital elements of human existence. Because a person tends to level out as he grows older, he often hems himself into channels of least resistance, and does not expend sufficient energy, enthusiasm, and drive to free himself. Many executives have discussed the problem of getting one of their men to visualize himself at a new level of activity. They believe a certain man may have great potential, but say that the ultimate drive must come from the man himself. That drive can come only through growth.

A desire to grow, to develop potential both vertically and horizontally, is the foundation for the development of a positive outlook and rewarding goals. Bob Hope, for example, continues in his seventies to realize his potential with undiminished vigor and will undoubtedly continue to do so as long as his health permits. Such an ideal provides a lifetime guide for action because it is continuous and never ending. One can only speculate as to the depth of human potential in the incredible story of Helen Keller, who became a great person in spite of being born blind, deaf, and dumb.

Realistically, what is the payoff for engaging in the process of realizing potential? In its total concept it involves the consideration of the mental, physical, and spiritual dimensions of life and the development of a whole man. It provides, therefore, a sound basis for self-fulfillment, and the realization of a person's extrinsic and intrinsic goals. The rewards can be great. It begins with a strong desire to project one's own unique abilities and capabilities through the kaleidoscope of human endeavor and accomplishment.

Component 2—Faith and Belief

The second major component of the positive mind is viewed as faith and belief in your self and your chosen work.

Countless people suffer throughout their lives from a lack of confidence in themselves. We are just learning from transactional analysis that our feelings of confidence are undermined in our early years of life and that unless we make a conscious decision to reject this self-negation and adopt faith in ourselves, we will suffer from feelings of inferiority all our lives. Psychiatrists seem to be saying that faith and belief, and the feelings we have about ourselves, tend to be negative unless we consciously construct our own positive viewpoint. The desire to grow, to get better and better, is the first step in building self-confidence. Norman Vincent Peale says in *The Power of Positive Thinking*:

Feelings of confidence depend upon the type of thoughts that habitually occupy your mind. Think defeat and you are bound to feel defeated, but practice thinking positive thoughts, make it a dominating habit, and you will develop such a strong sense of capacity that regardless of what difficulties arise you will be able to overcome them. Feelings of confidence actually induce increased strength.*

There can be no question of the extraordinary power that an individual has when he is confident of his own capacities or his own abilities, his own worth as a person. A man thus inspired has a leadership quality which stems from his confidence, and he is likely to have an impact on other lives. Faith and belief expressed by self-confidence develops enthusiasm, optimism, sincerity, energy, and commitment.

Key Conditioners

A number of simple associative phrases and sentences are used in this book in order to later recall key ideas which relate to the realization of potential. One of these sentences was made popular years ago by Dr. Émile Coué, the exponent of auto-suggestion, and many parents have used it: "Every day in every way I'm getting better and better." A simple analysis of this would be:

Every day (not just today, but tomorrow, next week, and all of the time)
In every way (in the way I look, think, and act)
I'm getting better and better (not just good, but much better than before, and there is improvement every day).

Continuous repetition of this sentence has a strong influence on a growing faith and belief in one's self.

A basic factor involved in strengthening faith in ourselves begins with an evaluation of what we are doing in life and how we feel about it. This evaluation *must be* based on truth. For example, anyone—businessman, housewife, student—who is

* Prentice-Hall, 1952, p. 138.

falling down on the job of running his life will have trouble maintaining and developing an appropriate degree of faith and belief in himself. Faith and self-confidence are based on a reasonably satisfying and effective life, and cannot be properly supported when one feels ashamed or apologetic about what one is doing. We need to put ourselves in a position where we can feel proud of what we're doing, and we need to become increasingly aware of our own achievements so that when we begin to rate ourselves on our own scale, we can begin to push our own personal marks up a bit higher each time we do it.

The subject of self-image will be dealt with at considerably greater length further on in Chapter 4, but the important point of the positive mind is that in order to sustain and develop self-confidence we need to be excited about ourselves and our growth. We see this in a man who has committed himself to a cause. He is the man other people will follow, for he believes in himself and in his cause. It is often interesting to observe a man who is new in a particular endeavor. Over a period of time he may begin to produce some very spectacular results, to the point where the old men around him will begin to ask what this particular man is doing to accomplish so much. Very often the answer is that he is doing exactly the same thing the older men are doing, but that the difference is his enthusiasm for what he is doing.

I believe that a man's maximum growth involves dedication to the total phenomenon of growth so that all components can function together and create the foundation for a satisfactory evaluation of one's self. The process of growing, of becoming, tends to destroy the atmosphere in which negative emotions breed. Most people who suffer from negative emotions do not understand that the solution to the problem lies not in an attack by the conscious mind on the specific problems of fear, worry, resentment, or envy, but rather in the development of their own potential in a positive, satisfying way by adoption of strong goals. A slight change in perspective, in understanding of ourselves, can dramatically alter a negative viewpoint.

There is another aspect of a growing faith in yourself that

can be most important and that is that, unless you have a positive mind and faith in yourself, you are apt to absorb negative emotions put out by other people and by the events which occur daily around you. This fact is important at all levels of life, for the human mind operates somewhat like a pendulum, constantly moving back and forth, from positive to negative, in its judgments and its views. For example, a person who is buying something of importance will look at the advantages of buying, and then will think of all the disadvantages. In the course of this appraisal, his mind may go back and forth ten times from positive to negative before he makes a decision. In the same way, we are constantly exposed in our family, business, and social lives to thoughts which alternate between positive and negative, and at times it takes strong faith and belief in one's self to continue to radiate positive, meaningful thoughts. If a person does not maintain faith in himself, he will begin to put out negative thought patterns to others in his daily life, and he will have little problem in receiving the same in return.

The ability to be positive, to grow, to stay young in spirit was commented upon in a beautiful way by General Douglas MacArthur: "Nobody grows old by merely living a number of years. People grow old by deserting their ideals. Years may wrinkle the skin, but to give up interest wrinkles the soul. Worry, doubt, self-distrust, fear and despair—these are the long, long years that bow the head and turn the growing spirit back to dust. Whatever your years, there is in every being the love of wonder, the undaunted challenge of events, the unfailing appetite for what next, and the joy and the game of life. You are as young as your ambition, as old as your doubt; as young as your self-confidence, as old as your fear; as young as your hope, as old as your despair."

Visualization

An important tool in the building of self-confidence and faith in ourselves lies in our capacity to visualize ourselves as being successful. Visualization of ourselves as worthwhile individuals who really amount to something is an important part of realizing potential. We become goal-oriented, and our minds will tend to move in the direction of what we are thinking about. If you think you're a failure, you probably will be. If you think you're a success, you very well may be.

The development of a self-confident image of ourselves as succeeding in our work and in our lives is a vital tool which is available for our use. Any person who plays a sport, whether it be golf, tennis, or bowling, knows what a lack of self-confidence can do to his game. The man who is confident of his own abilities has a chance to make a good shot consistent with his abilities, but his chances of success are slim if he lacks confidence. One of the major themes of this book will be to suggest methods and ways of using the imagination to visualize success.

In some mysterious way the mind uses and develops what we imagine, what we visualize, and a major factor in developing faith in ourselves is to literally saturate our minds, to immerse ourselves in thought processes which are positive. Expect the best and never think the worst. Concentrate on the best image in your mind, picture it, emphasize it, develop it, get excited about it to the point where you actually believe its realness, its meaning. You then make the possible become probable. Fill your mind with thoughts of faith, hope, courage, expectancy, even though the task of staying positive becomes more difficult. We are subjected to an increasing avalanche of bad news through the newspaper and television media: the energy crisis, unemployment, war, inflation, and on and on. For self-protection, many people are beginning to limit their intake of news because it can have an adverse effect on positive thinking. But these are transient distractions; all crises pass, and they cannot be allowed to affect our thought processes negatively when they occur. A basic objective is to take into our minds those thoughts which are positive and which express the best in us, and then to build meaning into our systems by concentrating and emphasizing and developing these mental images.

Positive Thinking

There is another simple key sentence which can be helpful in developing confidence in yourself and in developing a positive mind. The sentence is this: "Positive thoughts benefit me." Just as "every day I'm getting better and better" is associated with your desire to grow, "positive thoughts benefit me" can be associated with faith and belief in yourself. This statement should be given meaning through frequent repetition and through mental emphasis on its various aspects: *Positive thoughts* (the thoughts of optimism, faith, and belief in myself, enthusiasm, courage, hope) *benefit me* (the positive thoughts benefit my health; they can bring happiness, peace of mind; they are vital to my well-being, and they can aid me in achieving my goals in life). This key, "Positive thoughts benefit me," will help you recollect the advantages of positive thinking. The person who is thinking positively attracts positive forces which move him toward his goal. Make positive thinking your obsession, and let faith and belief in yourself and your work saturate your mind. Fill your mind with these thoughts, particularly before going to sleep at night. Most people who lose interest, who level out, are just not interested in anything. They live in a world bounded by their own worries and desires, and their energy level is low. "Positive thoughts benefit me" helps keep us pointed in the right direction.

Our View of Our Work

An important part of our self-confidence and our belief in ourselves relates to how we view the work that we do during the day. Most families in this country have to work for a living in order to be able to buy the things that money provides, and it is a common misconception on the part of many that happiness would come if their money needs were satisfied or that it will come at retirement when work is no longer necessary. The truth of the matter is that work is therapy of the finest kind, and people who have protracted periods of loafing and idleness soon find out that ease, comfort, and achieving all of one's goals is a state of boredom, not growth.

The impact of work on health and longevity was studied by the Metropolitan Life Insurance Company, and it was found that the death rate of top company executives was only 58 percent of the normal rate for men of their age. The researchers concluded that work satisfaction and public recognition may be an important determinant of health and longevity.

Dr. Richard Holton, dean of business administration at the University of California, said recently: ". . . he may seek real satisfaction with the content of his work. He may be willing to work longer hours for less income if he is 'doing his own thing.' He may want a great deal of variety in his life. . . . We may be in for a 'restructuring of our society.' "

The way a man views his work has a marked impact on his vertical achievement index and his feeling of worth. It can be exceptionally important for a young man to determine whether he really does not care for a particular job or whether his attitude would be the same in any job.

We all admire those who enjoy their jobs. The fact that they do is quite obvious. It has also been found that if one potentiality or strength is fully developed, it can trigger discovery of other areas of potential in life. Those who are dedicated to their work often develop their lives to an outstanding degree. Dedication to a high calling, to serving others, can provide about the best enjoyment we can have.

The person who decides he is going to work and that he is going to like it can often be good in a number of fields. He could, for example, probably be a good doctor, a good plumber, or a good teacher, but without the desire to do well in his chosen field, he will not be worth much in any of these fields. Many people suffer because they have no hunger for achievement, no particular taste for anything; yet man can live long and happily working along modest lines if he enjoys his work and is reasonably successful at it. A carpenter can have great satisfaction out of a well-made chair, a tailor out of a well-made suit, and a shoemaker from a pair of shoes that are admired. Only frustration and lack of purpose can spoil the performance. The individual who feels he is in a "calling" in his work has a great advantage in life. The housewife, while rearing four children, may at times doubt her "calling," but she is engaged in a vital and rewarding task. The doctor, lawyer, creative salesman, or skilled craftsman is usually engaged in a "calling," but unfortunately may lose sight of this fact. A person with such a viewpoint has a mission in life and a purpose, and people can sense it. An example of a man in a "calling" is Billy Graham, who is so fiery in his dedication that he draws people from miles around to hear him preach. His talents are concentrated because he is devoted to his mission.

When a person is able to feel that his work is worthwhile and satisfying, he has added a most vital ingredient to the process of his growth.

One important cause to which one may dedicate himself when he feels that he is in a "calling" lies in the concept of serving people primarily, with only secondary regard for personal compensation. It is axiomatic that in the giving of yourself you get back more than you receive, and this applies to every part of life. A very successful motivator of men used to say that man should be trained to be go-givers rather than go-getters. The concept of being a go-giver first is a practical one in business terms, for it is based on the fact that in helping one person there may be no financial reward, but in helping many the reward may be substantial. Men who intensely believe this philosophy are often those who rise to great heights in their professions. The desire to "serve first," to be a go-giver, is in essence the golden rule, and its impact on the positive side is considerable.

The theme of this book lies in the fulfillment of a person to the point where he enjoys life because he is in the process of developing his many potentials to better serve. A man may work for money, or he may not, but the principles of self-fulfillment remain the same. A great modern leader of men recently said, "A man never levels-out giving," and all outgoing people can ponder, understand, and respect the wisdom of these words.

Money and Potential

Fulfillment is too often thought of in terms of money and possessions, or in what money can buy. The pressure for creature comforts is so intense that many men will dedicate their lives to making money. The principles in this book have been proved beyond doubt to develop a man's potential and hence his ability to earn more than he otherwise would. The earning of money is vitally important to the family structure, and the dedication of a man to his business and to the accumulation of an estate is appropriate and necessary. But to be truly successful, it should be done from the standpoint of wholeness, from a man's realization of his complete growth as a person.

Arthur Rubenstein, the world-renowned pianist, said, "During my long life I have learned one lesson: The most important thing is to realize why one is alive—and I think it is not only to build bridges or tall buildings or make money, but to do something truly important, to do something for humanity. To bring joy, hope, to make life richer for the spirit because you have been alive, that is the most important thing."

Money, as a commodity in itself, can be either helpful or detrimental to an individual. The young person who inherits money and who then assumes he "has it made" can shortly harm himself. On the other hand, money can be a lever for the development of other potentials that we have. A recent television special on the lives of the Rockefeller brothers eloquently illustrated this point. Each of these men is totally dedicated to a career in which he works ten to fifteen hours a day. Their money has enabled them to select the work they want to do, and when starting at the bottom, to be almost immediately at the top. In addition to enjoying their work, they are able to surround themselves with people they like who assist them. In this case, money avoids many of the normal frustrations of life and opens up avenues of achievement for these very fine men, which would otherwise not be available. The Rockefellers' need is certainly not to earn money, but to live up to their potential, which is the same problem the nonwage earner has.

Most people are working at jobs that are necessary, yet not inspiring or absorbing, but many manage to achieve full lives by maximizing creative thoughts in their work, by interest in their fellow workers, by their outside interests, and through the learning process. Not everyone can be president of the company, but a man can learn to enjoy his work, if he chooses to do so. In terms of the positive mind, the decision to look positively at one's work is of first-rate importance.

In the life insurance business, for example, a man can look at the job of selling in two ways. The first approach is that he is talking to a man who doesn't want to see him, who doesn't want to buy anything, and that he is talking about an event (death) the man does not want to think about. The second approach is that he has a golden opportunity to directly serve people on a one-to-one basis and to see firsthand how he can help. He feels that he fulfills a vital need and that he can run his own business and be well rewarded because of his service. Men with the first approach do poorly while those dedicated to service succeed beyond their expectations.

Once a man fully experiences the satisfaction of serving others through the development of his own unique potential, he can never turn back. He develops an exquisite awareness of what is to be done and what can be done. While his motives may at times be questioned by others, he is not driven by fear, the need to conform, or the sole drive for accumulation. He has touched upon the core of his being, and he cannot then retreat back into comfortable complacency. Through his own growth, he begins to sense the exhilaration of being a complete person.

The act of transcending one's self can be illustrated by two violinists of equal technical ability who play the same composition. One musician is totally absorbed in playing the notes, and he knows that he is playing them correctly. His performance is technically perfect, but it is not alive. The other violinist loses himself in the music. He does not just finger the strings but lets the music flow through him, and the audience loves what they hear because his performance is true and because the music springs spontaneously from his being. He literally becomes the music and does not simply perform it. He has transcended himself.

Component 3—Positive Response to Pressure

The third element of the positive mind is a positive response to pressure. Every part of this book relates in one way or another to this challenge.

The ability to respond positively to the stresses of our daily lives is of critical importance. Essentially, such a response involves our ability to meet the ups and downs of the day with courage, determination, cheerfulness, equanimity, and challenge. A negative response to pressure involves emotions of anxiety, fear, discouragement, disappointment, and frustration.

The ability to respond positively and appropriately to stress is of far-reaching importance because no person is immune to the pressures and stresses of life. Every individual has to face crises in his work and in his family life. He must face the potential loss of loved ones, illness, and eventually his own death. But these stresses and strains are a part of any normal, functioning life. As a matter of fact, no one would seriously want to eliminate pressure from life, for there is nothing more pathetic than the old person who is little more than a vegetable. There is a great need for a system in life which will enable a person to respond positively to pressure. Problems accumulate over the years and flexibility in handling those problems can diminish. If a person is not in the process of growth, a consistently negative response to pressure may be encouraged.

It is well known that there is a direct relationship between our emotions and our physical health, and it has been estimated that at least one-half of all illnesses is induced by the emotions. Emotions, which represent a negative response to pressure, operate over a long period of time and are much more dangerous than most infectious illnesses, from which we recover in a matter of weeks. The range of emotionally induced illnesses covers the whole spectrum of health care, but some obvious diseases which may be caused by stress are ulcers, high blood pressure, and heart disease. A key element in stress is its origin in our mental attitudes, for unless we respond and react to pressure, nothing happens. For example, if we pass someone on the street who has insulted us, nothing happens if we ignore him. If we stop and seek a fight, aside from physical injury, we increase our heart rate, raise our blood pressure, and change the chemistry of our body in a way that is dangerous. Continued upset of the nervous system, where we react negatively, eventually causes disease.

More and more medical reports verify the detrimental effects of stress. A recent article stated: "A study of 505 middle-aged men in Helsinki, Finland, who either survived a heart attack or died from one, showed that about two-thirds experienced stressful life changes within a year before their attacks. The life changes that increased the stress level ranged from death of a wife to a traffic ticket. Many researchers are coming to regard chronic stress as a potent hazard to the body which can not only cause damage directly, as in an ulcer, but also can precipitate the appearance of other diseases." The medical profession is continuously documenting the detrimental effects of long-range stress on the human system. Their message to a layman is very clear: If you hope to live a reasonably long and happy life, you must learn to respond positively to stress.

Dr. Hans Selye, in his article "Stress and the Executive," says:

Each period of stress, especially if it results from frustrating, unsuccessful struggles, leaves some irreversible chemical scars which accumulate to constitute the signs of tissue aging. But successful activity, no matter how intense, leaves virtually no such scars. On the contrary, it provides you with the exhilarating feeling of youthful strength, even at a very advanced age. *

Stress in Business

Creative people seem to fall into several groups, each group with different problems and stresses. The first group reaches a certain financial level which is sufficient to enable them to live in an acceptable life-style. Even though they are operating at a point well below their capacity and are aware of this, they have reached a point where they don't know what to do about it. They may lack the knowledge and the purposes and desire for self-motivation, or they may be locked into a job situation, and they are at an impasse. People is this group adapt to this fact, and do not suffer stress in its true sense. They know that something is missing and would do something about it if they could, but they don't worry about it. This group is not a cop-out; its members are well-adjusted to the facts of life, as they see it. They may well develop their potential horizontally.

The second group is identical with the first, with one exception: These people may be frustrated by their inability to progress beyond a certain point. They are aware of their limitations, but they may be unable to accept the fact that they have leveled out. They find some refuge in substitutes, but stress becomes a part of their lives, because of their frustration over their potential gap. On the scale of 0 to 10, they may rate themselves a 5 or 6.

A third group can suffer severe stress because they try to operate out of the range of their real capabilities. The attempt to achieve excellence can be overdone to the point where an individual goes well over his stress level, and this type of stress often leads to physical or mental breakdown. The person in this group may be in a job or family situation for which he is totally unsuited, and which, for him, involves great tension. A friend who recently had a nervous breakdown told me on the telephone, "Bob, I just found out after 20 years, I'm in the

* Executive Publications, 1973.

wrong business." A recent article in the *Chicago Tribune* was titled "Job Market Beckons but Youth Needs Guidance." It said, "All over the country young people seem to be asking for help; many believe they have somehow lost control of the direction and management of their lives." "Our son is totally unsure of his future," laments one parent. "His school offers him nothing as far as guidance [is concerned]. We've made many calls to the superintendent of education and have met with no encouragement." As I have said, the ability to enjoy one's work is crucial to the positive mind; the importance of early career guidance cannot be overestimated, but unfortunately it is well below par. As indicated by my friend who had the breakdown, the selection of a person's work should begin early in life and it should be thorough.

I know another group of men who are dedicated to their jobs and who are growing. I have observed that these two qualities, dedication and growth, enable these men to respond in a positive way to pressure. I don't mean to say that this group has fewer problems. They have more! But their activity is so great that they develop the capacity to "roll with the punches." If a real estate man has ten listings and he loses four of them, he may well suffer stress. If he has a hundred listings and loses four, he has no stress, for obvious reasons. One of the most important goals of the process of realizing potential is to enable a man to respond positively to pressure.

Stress and tension materially affect our performance in life, for tension inhibits the creative powers of the mind. The ability of the mind to utilize information, to coordinate that information with current thinking, and to compute accurate responses depends on a relaxed, free-flowing mind. The professional golfer or concert pianist cannot possibly perform at his best if he is tense. The television programs of Perry Como and Bing Crosby are outstanding examples of relaxed performances which are totally effective and which do not project tension. Tension is communicated to others, and at times it is almost as if people are tuned in on the same wavelength. Responses made in such an atmosphere will be strained and awkward. For example, a man who badly needs money from a particular effort cannot possibly perform as a professional. His responses are formulated on the basis of his need rather than on doing the job, and his feelings will be sensed.'

Tension also disperses energy and therefore lowers output. A relaxed person can more readily focus his energies toward the important areas of his life and he conserves his nervous energy. The professional baseball pitcher is an outstanding example of relaxation and the complete coordination of mind and body. He releases the ball at the precise moment that all of his mental and physical forces produce their greatest power. The professional golfer releases his power in the last two feet of his downward swing. If he is uptight the power of this release is destroyed because his mental and physical processes are not coordinated.

Creative ability is beyond our power of conscious control. Its release depends upon actions which have gone before; it depends on the information and thoughts which the individual has put into his mind as he lives each day. Tension and stress inhibit this process and make it impossible for creativity to function properly. The free-flowing operation of our creative mind is necessary to the purpose of achieving our potential and to the development of our specific goals.

Stress Suppressal Techniques

As the dangers of stress become more clear, techniques for developing a positive response to pressure are available. A major part of the problem of a negative response is that we overrespond to what we see and hear, which can then induce the emotions of fear, worry, and anger. Much of this response is unnecessary because it represents our interpretation of an event rather than the subjective effect of the event itself.

For example, some years ago a young man was to speak before an audience of over a thousand people. The thought of doing this disturbed him physically, and a friend advised him that if he experienced difficulty when he took his place at the speaker's lectern, he should take a few deep breaths; if he still felt frightened, he should step back slightly, take another deep breath, and then begin to talk. The young man finally stepped up before this group of people to make his speech. He found himself so frightened that he was unable to talk, so he stepped back and took a deep breath and resumed his place. He found that he still could not talk and he stepped back again, took some more deep breaths, and stepped forward, but again his fear had immobilized him. When he stepped back the third time, he moved a little farther, and disappeared from the audience, as the platform was raised and was open in the back. Needless to say, the incident was never forgotten, and I was told on good authority that this young man later went on from this point to overcome this fear, this overresponse, and that he became an outstanding speaker.

Much of the stress of life lies in the fact that we do over-respond because of what we imagine as true about a particular situation, and most of the negative things we imagine either are not true or never happen. Experts point out that a negative response causes actual chemical changes in the body which predispose a person to illness, but that the effect varies with each person because of his heredity, his habits, his health, and his individual reactions. From a layman's viewpoint, this consistent negative response is so harmful that when we persist in overreacting negatively, we can help ourselves avoid it if we imagine that we are orally taking a very detrimental drug. If we can learn to let go, to not react excessively, we can virtually eliminate stress as a physically detrimental agent. In other words, you can't eliminate stress, but you can minimize it by controlling overreaction that induces physiological changes in the nervous system.

One of my friends told me about one of the simplest specifics for the release of tension. He said, "I don't know why, but when I think of the past I always think of the good things." The capacity to think of the pleasant things of life and to concentrate on goals that will improve us is one of the most efficient ways of assuring a positive response to pressure.

A most insidious problem of the businessman is the feeling of being hurried. Its origins can be in a compulsive pursuit for perfection or, more likely, in a disorganized or ill-conceived schedule. It leads to a harried, worried existence which is extremely detrimental to the use of potential. Hurry and worry destroy peace of mind and make tremendous inroads on business efficiency. An associative phrase to remind one of this trap is "no hurry—no worry." The point is that a well-planned leisurely schedule does eliminate most worries.

Relaxation

Physical relaxation is essential to avoiding overresponse. The concept of the coordination of mind and body of the athlete clearly shows the relationship of physical relaxation and tension, and the professional athlete destroys that coordination as soon as stress and tension develop. Physical relaxation counters tension and therefore negative thinking. Worry, fear, and anxiety do not exist in the brain alone, but as residual tension patterns throughout the body, which continues long after you think you have relaxed. Recent studies show that when an individual imagines in his mind that he is doing something, he actually carries out the act in his muscles, a reaction so slight that only very sensitive instruments can detect and register it. It appears that brain activity and muscular activity are interdependent, and residual tension can create a vicious cycle of mind acting on muscle, and vice versa, until operating under tension becomes a way of life.

The eye muscles are a most important factor in residual tension. It has been demonstrated that when people close their eyes and picture objects in their minds, the eye muscles contract as though they were actually looking at the object. When they open their eyes, the eye muscles relax and the mental image vanishes. However, the ability to close the eyes, blank out visual images, and relax the eye muscles is important to complete physical relaxation. Practiced relaxation stops mental imagery and hence the visualization of problems; when the mind ceases its activity, an individual gains an important degree of mental control. Physical relaxation provides a physiological rest for every part of the body and is an acquired skill. It involves training the muscles to act as you want them to act so that you can relax anytime, anywhere.

A negative response to stress is usually caused by the nature of our own response and not by external events. If we remain completely relaxed physically, a negative response will not occur because our images and our feelings of a negative nature are not transmitted to our bodies. The fact that we cannot feel anxious, fearful, or angry when our bodies are perfectly relaxed has been proved scientifically. Maxwell Maltz, in his book *Psycho-Cybernetics*, says:

Physical relaxation plays a key role in the de-hypnotization process. Our currently held beliefs, whether good or bad, true or false, were formed without effort, with no sense of strain, and without the exercise of 'will power.' Our habits, whether good or bad, were formed in the same way. It follows that we must employ the same process in forming new beliefs, or new habits, that is, in a relaxed condition. . . . By relaxing and maintaining a relaxed attitude, you remove those excessive states of concern, tension and anxiety which interfere with the operation of your creative mechanism. In time, your relaxed attitude will become a habit, and you will no longer need to consciously practice it.*

The first step is to fight unhealthy tension at all times. The professional in any endeavor has trained himself to respond positively to pressure, and he is capable of total physical relaxation at any time during the day. This art is a part of his life.

There are certain basic relaxation techniques which can be used by the businessman to acquire a relaxed attitude either as a regular exercise or for occasional use.

1. Breathing. Take a deep breath through the nostrils and hold it to the count of 3. Then expel it through the mouth. This breathing exercise is used extensively in Yoga for the purpose of renewing energy.

* Prentice-Hall, 1960, p. 59.

2. The eyes. Because of mental imagery, the eyes are an important factor in tension. Tell yourself to relax your eyelids and let the feeling descend through your entire body.

3. Visualization. Close your eyes and imagine that you are lying on a hospital bed with an attractive nurse in attendance. Imagine that your body is filled with air and that there are plugs in your legs and arms. Visualize the nurse pulling one plug at a time and feel the air go out of each limb. You may also visualize a very relaxing scene, that is, the surface of a lake, or a lovely garden.

4. Suggestion. Count down from 10 to 0 slowly, and at each count tell yourself you're becoming more deeply relaxed.

For example, to use the entire program, get comfortably seated. Close your eyes and breathe deeply to the count of 3. Relax your eyelids and feel that relaxation seeping down to your toes. Then imagine that the nurse is releasing the air out of your body. At that point, count down from 10 to 0, telling yourself that your relaxation is becoming deeper on each count.

You should sharpen your alertness to recognize early stress symptoms. You should try to avoid those situations to which we respond negatively. If you know that a certain activity tends to be stressful, you should try to anticipate it. For example, it is not difficult to ruin an entire day if you are in a bad humor in the morning. Saying things that you don't mean can lead to an argument which sets the tone for the whole day.

We can deliberately eliminate most negative responses by anticipating the problem, but it's up to us individually to determine our own stress levels. There are no pat answers, but we can create a frame of reference to work out our stress reactions. We need a purpose; we must have worthwhile goals and a positive mind and self-image if we are to work successfully with this problem. We must be successful, not only in our work, but in our lives. Nothing in the world is more conducive to longevity and health than to be successful. Nothing is more destructive than to be frustrated, to be beaten by a negative response to our jobs or to our families.

We spend a lifetime building financial security. We create pension plans, savings accounts, social security, and other benefits. Through achieving self-fulfillment, we also build a bank account of inner strength, of usefulness, goodwill, love, and self-respect. These assets are a permanent reservoir which is constantly added to, and which cannot be taken away as money and power can be. These are the assets we need when real crises occur, when we need a positve response to pressure.

We have to learn to let ourselves go, to relax anytime, anywhere, without drugs. A relaxed condition enables us to be competitive but with a positive response to pressure, which strengthens the well-adjusted personality. There is probably nothing in the world more relaxed than a cat quietly sitting or lying down with its eyes half-closed in a state of total relaxation. But, let a mouse run by, and like a streak of lightning the cat pounces. A cat wastes no movements, and we can learn much from it about the conservation of energy.

As you go through the day, observe yourself at frequent intervals. Try to catch yourself wasting energy through nervous habits and tensed muscles. When this happens, calmly order all tense muscles to relax, and don't be afraid to repeat the order.

A positive response to pressure can be learned and developed, but the touch can also be lost. A man who scores himself high in terms of his potential index is almost invariably responding well to pressure.

Being Positive and a Low Achievement Level

The realistic and sometimes harsh facts of business life often involve periods of time when business is bad. Profits may be nonexistent or severe losses may occur. This can be an unpleasant and trying period for any man at any level of business. At this point an achievement index figure of 7 or 8 can easily slip to a 5.

As noted before, when a man is locked into a job which he

feels does not use his potential, he may be unable to rise above a 4 or 5 level. And there are also those who feel they have more potential but who are unable to activate it and who may remain at a 5 level.

From the standpoint of the positive mind, the problem is obvious. A low rating can begin to induce a negative response to pressure. Feelings of fear, anger, apathy (to name but a few) begin to take over. In turn, this affects one's faith and belief. And finally a man can begin to believe his doubts and doubt his beliefs. Unless he is in the process of realizing his potentials, he may well succumb to this vicious cycle. The price tag in terms of his effectiveness and emotional well-being can be too great.

The solution presented in this book is to integrate the components of the positive mind with a series of other components which can enable a man to respond positively when the going gets rough.

One of my good friends has put his life savings in his business of making steel poles. For two years he has been close to losing everything. He told me recently, "At times I could cry; the problems are so mammoth you know you're whipped. You've got to walk away to get your strength and then come back. Quitting limits the time, because it works out if you give it time. You're stalling for time and this can't happen if you quit. You wait until the referee blows the whistle, you don't blow it yourself." While this man's problems are unusually severe, the point of the story is that when a man's rating slips, he doesn't blow the whistle on himself by a negative response to pressure.

Summary

How do you live up to your potential? The very idea of realizing potential suggests that we are engaged in a rather predictable cycle of developing our energy and our intellect according to our particular talents and interests. This concept assumes that man does control his own destiny and that he decides the course he will follow on the basis of workable principles rather than chance. He then hopefully begins to motivate himself, to fulfill himself, and to maximize his enjoyment of life through helping others.

In the development of the positive mind we use three techniques. All three are needed because if negative thought processes have been imprinted on the mind, it will play these

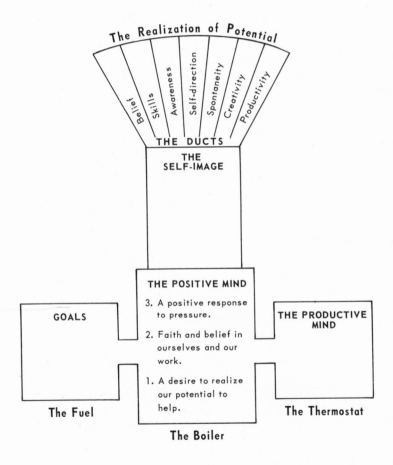

records over and over again until they have become habitual. Negative thinking is an entrenched enemy that can fight back viciously and will win unless we use every possible technique to dislodge it.

The first technique is that of association with other ideas, for this is perhaps the best way to remember something. For example, we associate our desire to realize potential with the key conditioning sentence "every day in every way I'm getting better and better." Our own self-confidence and getting the most out of our work is associated with "positive thoughts benefit me." A positive response to stress is associated with "no hurry—no worry." To dramatize the influence on our health when we continue an excessive negative response to pressure, we imagine that we are ingesting a dangerous chemical. The thought, for example, of heroin is so repugnant that its association with negative thought processes can be most effective.

The second technique is the saturation of the mind with positive thoughts and responses. Negative thoughts are always ready to take over, and unless we practice thought saturation long enough to make new records and establish new habits, we will slip back, inevitably, into negative responses. This is where it does not pay to be bashful. Tell yourself constantly that you're great (not, of course, egotistically), that you've done a fine job for your family and others, and that you can be proud of what you've done. Keep at it day after day, month after month, until you know beyond a doubt that it's true (and it is).

The third technique, and the one that takes over on a permanent basis, is the process toward realization itself, which was outlined in the first chapter. The positive components of the mind must be cultivated and used, and this involves goals to activate and give direction to the positive mind. For example, our goals can determine our stress level or how we feel about our work or ourselves. Properly used, goals weld together the components of the positive mind and can provide the power with which we can motivate ourselves to begin to realize our many potentials.

The finest way in the world to develop positive response to

pressure, self-confidence, and our purpose is through action which expresses our love and our help to others—right now, this minute. Presto! We eliminate pressure. But we need action, which is achieved through structuring and coordinating our goals with the elements of the positive mind. We need to prepare ourselves to help.

3

Checkpoint 2 — goals

In talking with businessmen about their future plans for themselves and their families, almost invariably these goals have been expressed in monetary terms. In the event he dies, the younger businessman wants his family to continue to live more or less as they do now. If he lives, he wants sufficient income with which to retire comfortably. In many cases his goals center around his company benefits; that is, his group life, medical, disability, and pension and savings benefits. He wants income currently with which to educate his children and live according to a certain standard of living now. Most often he wants to progress in his work so he can have additional money for his current and future needs—to travel, to create an estate, or perhaps to build a second home.

When a man either creates or inherits substantial capital, his attention turns to conserving and investing his money. If he dies, he wants to pay Uncle Sam as little as necessary in taxes. If he lives, he wants to maximize his return through investment in tax-free bonds, or leveraged real estate, or some form of tax shelter.

External goals for the businessman are usually related to money, and sometimes to the desire for prestige and power. A desire to seek potential vertically is necessary if a man is to earn the money his talent, drive, and circumstances permit. Out of the desire to grow vertically, the businessman begins to develop his own goals and his own problems. Recently, in discussing the process of developing potential with several men about age 40, I found that their interest was almost entirely in vertical growth, and appropriately so, because each had a large family and considerable overhead. These men had all of the usual money objectives, but I was struck with their deep desire to develop their business potential. As far as income was concerned, they were doing very well, with an average yearly income of about $30,000. Yet when they rated the use of their potential on the scale of 0 to 10, the appraisal in each case was at about a level of 5. Their general feeling could be expressed as follows: "I'm doing well financially, but I somehow don't feel good about it. I just don't feel I'm living up to my abilities."

In terms of external goals, these men do well. But in terms of their intrinsic goals—their self-esteem, confidence, competence, and inner worth—they are suffering. This condition exists with many men, but it is not apparent on the surface. This type of individual finds the process of realizing potential especially rewarding because it provides a philosophy of growth, as well as key checkpoints, for his personal use. In most cases this is all he needs to continue his development on a positive basis.

In terms of potential, the thrust of this book lies in the development of potential vertically in a man's work to the limit of his abilities and desires, with potential then also being used horizontally in his daily life. There are those whose dedication to their work is so complete that there may be little time left for other pursuits. As a man grows vertically, his responsibilities as well as his income tend to increase, and the demands on his vertical potential also increase.

This contrasts with a recent study of automobile workers engaged in production-line work, reported in an issue of *Archives of General Psychiatry,* which provides fascinating insight into the development of horizontal potential. It has been widely assumed that repetitive jobs produce boredom and life dissatisfaction. The authors of the article said, "To impute boredom, alienation, or the seeds of mental illness to another man's work or existence is a hazardous thing. . . . Living in stable neighborhoods, they have effectively seized control over their own destiny and security through the powerful yet highly democratic union. The job is not the center of their lives, or its source of meaning, but a means toward enjoyment of other pursuits and security." In terms of business goals, the auto worker needs none. His work is fixed and repetitive. His goals, therefore, are personal ones.

As a businessman progresses, however, his business goals become more demanding, more creative, and more difficult. His compensation will generally reflect the degree of difficulty of his work. While his business goals may be set for him, he has latitude in the methods to achieve them, and they tend to be forcing, and demanding. The mix of the businessman's vertical and horizontal potential is entirely an individual decision.

While each man decides his own mix of vertical and horizontal potential, the ultimate goal must be development of a balanced or whole man who functions well in or out of a business environment.

Goals Are Where the Action Is

The positive mind is in suspension until you think or do something. You can't respond to pressure if there is no pressure; you can't be self-confident if you're doing nothing. But the moment a thought or a desire or a goal is visualized, the spotlight of the mind focuses on it, and begins to work toward it. Goals activate and give meaning to the positive mind and the purpose of realizing potential.

In the business world, goal setting is becoming an increasingly sophisticated procedure, generally called "management by objective." There is unquestionably a great need for strong forcing systems such as this, for self-motivation continues to be an art used by a relatively small percentage of men, and company-structured goals and careful follow-up keep us on the track. The development of potential involves the need for external forcing systems, but depends on the internal growth of a man for the true support of external motivators.

For example, assume that Joe and Jim are managers in similar departments, or perhaps salesmen selling the same product in the same territory. Assume that both men work under the same circumstances in their business, that they have the same basic family background, and that they both earned a master's degree in business from Harvard University. Because of the identical nature of their situations, the goals set for them are identical, yet Joe's record is far superior to Jim's, year after year. If superficial differences are swept aside, there are two underlying reasons for this variance in performance.

First, in Joe's case, his business goals are his and not someone else's. Joe evaluates his business goals in terms of the opportunity to increase his income and to progress further in his job, and he recognizes and values the inner feelings of growth which for him take the form of pride, a sense of belonging, a feeling of competency, and a sense of inner worth. He is aware that these feelings depend on how he feels about his goals.

The second difference between Joe and Jim is that in Joe's case his business goals have deep meaning to him. Because of the depth of this meaning, his progress toward his goals accelerates. Joe uses, either consciously or unconsciously, a variety of techniques which assist him in developing the meaning of his goals. (Certain of these techniques, and visualization in particular, are covered in this chapter.) In addition to specific techniques, Joe has a strong desire to achieve his potential through striving to become what he is capable of becoming. From this basic purpose he develops his dreams and his personal goals, which then motivate him.

In Jim's case, his thoughts are really not much different from Joe's, but unlike Joe he is not totally committed to his goals and they are less important to him. His results clearly reflect his lack of commitment, the lack of meaning of his goals!

One of the central themes of the process of developing potential is that a man should have goals that are truly his own and that they should have deep meaning for him. One of my friends with a large company has the responsibility for a substantial group of men. In discussing this matter with him he said, "How do you get a man to make goals his own?" While the answer to this question underlies the theme of this book, I have observed over the years that when a man is exposed to a leader who understands the process of growth and who is personally committed to it, he can often be lifted to a new level of achievement. At the present time, such leaders are rare in any business endeavor. They are able to transmit to others the meaning and message of growth. Such a man believes in himself, and he believes in the man he is talking to. His sincerity and enthusiasm are contagious. He has the capacity to challenge men to accept goals and to make them his own because his message springs from the center of his being. He is successful in getting men to accept difficult goals as their own because he has literally transcended himself. One of these rare leaders of men said to me recently, "When I'm hiring a man for our sales force, I don't look for the star. I want an average, intelligent man I can take from the level he's now at to a much higher level of competence." His record in developing men is superb.

One answer to getting a man to make company goals his own is through a great leader. The other, and much more obvious, answer is for a man to learn to motivate himself through the process of realizing his own potentials.

Introduction to Goal Setting

To a businessman the setting of goals is such a normal part of doing business that the subject would hardly seem worth reexploring, yet this is far from the truth. In discussing potential with me, the son of a friend said, "You mentioned the various stations where you can board the round-trip potential train. If you were starting out, where would you get on?" I replied, "My target would be goal structuring, because it is virtually impossible to get off the track if you structure your goals in the right way." A man who is goal-oriented, and who keeps his goals in balance, has a clear-cut plan for his life. For the sophisticated businessman, goal structuring is routine, but keeping business goals in balance with personal goals on a continuing basis is a permanent challenge.

It is well known that if goals are to be fully effective, they need to be positive, challenging, realistic, and very clearly defined. Most importantly, they have to mean a great deal to us, and they should be our goals and not somebody else's. Positive, meaningful goals do one other thing: They continuously reinforce the basic purpose of growth and the realization of our potential. The reverse side of the coin is that a deep desire to realize potential automatically causes a man to seek worthwhile goals.

Purpose and Goals

The purpose of realizing in life one's own unique potential is in itself a goal which is never achieved. It is, in a sense, a direction one takes in his life and not a destination, for human potential is great and one can hardly begin to explore it fully in a lifetime. The development of such a noble purpose automatically means that an individual structures satellite goals in his work, in his family and social life, in his community and spiritual life so as to continuously grow and increasingly live the good life.

The ability to properly structure goals is essential to realizing our potential. The purpose of realizing our potential is all-encompassing; it is three-dimensional in nature and covers the physical, mental, and spiritual potentials of a person. Goals, on the other hand, are ordinarily specific and have limited objectives which can cover any part of the three dimensions of purpose. For example, a man may have as a goal a salary of $25,000 a year; a family may want to take a trip to Europe; or a parent may want to set up a fund for the college education of his children. Many people have as their goal the accumulation of money or status and power; or a man may wish to develop his skill in a sport and to develop his body physically.

A fascinating aspect of goal structuring is its benefit to

those people who have a purpose for their lives, but who may severely restrict their goals. Yet, the ability to live fully and renew one's self is best achieved by having a large purpose and large goals. When a man fully commits himself to discovering his many potentials, he can begin to develop into something larger than himself; he can begin to transcend himself. This is sometimes observable in people who feel they have a high calling and who have such a talent for living the full life. The most meaningful goals can be sought when an individual finds his place in the scheme of things and when he regards his own life as meaningful. Herbert A. Otto, in his book *A Guide for Developing Your Potential,* says, "There is every reason to conclude that lack of purpose in life, and the absence of clearly formulated goals which transcend the narrow scope of the individual are deeply inimical to the development of potential." * The beginning of the discovery of our own potential to serve and to grow provides the best kind of enjoyment we can have in our lives. There isn't time to be bored because it's like drilling and finding an inexhaustible source of energy which enables a man to live each moment to its fullest.

Goals and Growth

Goals give meaning to the purpose of growth. Through goal structuring, we become responsible for what happens in our lives. Goal structuring develops with practice, and it is a technique which involves taking charge of our lives, perhaps requiring a profound change in habits and life-style. The setting of goals is a matter for each individual to determine for himself, for each of us has a priceless right to utilize our own experience in our own way and to develop our own particular talents. People differ in their goals because what fulfills one man will not fulfill another. There are, for example, large numbers of people in this country who will never desire more than the health and well-being of their own families, and there

* Wilshire Book Co., 1967, p. 117.

are others whose primary interest in life is in what their hands can produce, and these people will make a real contribution to society.

In the setting of goals we take charge of our lives. Instead of drifting aimlessly, we steer a course. The structuring of goals is like a road map which puts the individual in charge. Determining goals may at first be difficult, but once the skill is developed, it turns into a habit. Strong goals give us the opportunity to dream big dreams and to imagine where we will be at some point in the future. Somewhere I read, "Reach high, for stars lie hidden in our soul. Dream deep, for every dream precedes the goal." The person who wrote this not only was a good poet, but also knew a great deal about goal structuring.

A very successful businessman said to me recently, "I get my fun out of working toward a goal. Once I achieve the goal I lose interest." Isn't this the essence of not leveling out, of not attempting to perpetuate the present to the point where we cease to grow? Goal structuring involves movement toward something. A business associate commented to me, "Do you know, when I begin to get bored I look at this in a positive way. My mind is telling me that it is time to start growing again, to begin to set new and challenging goals."

No discussion of goal structuring would be complete without first considering the way in which the human mind automatically seeks to achieve whatever goals we supply to it.

Goals and the Nature of the Mind

Our most important single advantage in setting goals is that we are basically created as goal-striving beings in that our brains and nervous systems act automatically to achieve a certain goal. The science of cybernetics points out that the mind operates like a guided missile, which zeros in on a target and corrects course as it proceeds on its way. As we feed information and thoughts into our minds, our mental computer evaluates the information, processes it, and formulates an appropriate response. The mind remembers this response, whether it be a simple act like brushing our teeth or learning to drive an automobile, and at some point the response becomes a habit so that no further conscious thought is required. The important point is that the process works automatically and without regard for whether or not the results are good, bad, or indifferent. Positive, strong goals bring physical, emotional, and financial rewards. Nonspecific, lukewarm goals can be destructive and lead to the harmful nonuse of potential.

When a person sets strong, positive goals, his mind supplies the necessary energy, corrects the course through trial and error, then works its way toward the attainment of the goal. The man who wants something with every fiber of his being will be a difficult man to stop because he will develop great enthusiasm and energy toward accomplishing his goal.

Our minds seek to achieve our goals automatically and impersonally, and in addition our imaginations develop and embellish the picture of any particular goal. For example, if our goal is to build a new home, we automatically begin to think in terms of the type of home it should be, the interior layout and construction, where the money's coming from to build it, and on and on. In other words, because of our reactions to what we imagine about a particular experience, we proceed automatically and impersonally toward the goal.

Because of these facts, we have two vital tools for use in structuring our goals. The first is the knowledge that the entire process is automatic once we have thought of a particular objective, and the second is that, through our imagination, we can develop both our desire and the steps necessary to achieve it. Because the mind works automatically in seeking a solution to our problems, it can be a good friend or a deadly enemy, depending on the goals we implant in it. The mind which is not goal-oriented tends to drift aimlessly, and aimlessness does not utilize potential. Our explorative nature and the ability to consciously use our imagination in seeking our goals is a powerful lever in the process of realizing our own potential. We can deliberately set as a target the development of our positive mind, and we can imagine ourselves as being successful at our job and enjoying it, and we can see ourselves as being self-confident. We can set as a target our own personal growth and imagine what it would be like to be successfully moving ahead each day.

We have a priceless opportunity to select meaningful goals and then, by vividly visualizing what it would be like to achieve a particular goal, utilize the automatic processes of the mind to work toward its attainment. The proper use of this ability is vital to the realization of potential, and many references will be made to the technique of visualization. A senior executive said to me recently, "One of the most difficult things for a man to do is to imagine himself at a new level of competence. And yet this is what he must do if he is to move ahead in this company. It is perfectly obvious to us when a man feels himself to be at a new level, for everything he does at that point seems to correspond to this new picture he has of himself. If he just continues along his customary road, we may never give him a second glance."

Life Planning

If a man's purpose is to realize his potential to live fully —to fulfill himself—then sound structuring of major life goals would seem to logically follow. However, important goals can often be vague, not well defined, and not related to other goals. Because of this, many of the benefits of goal structuring can be lost. It seems that very few people ever sit down with a pencil and paper and write down their major life goals.

Lack of planning usually occurs because a man is caught up in current living. He establishes a life-style which appears to be reasonably satisfactory, but because of the pressures of work and other activities he may give little or no conscious thought to the overall direction his life should take and to his real needs. Unfortunately, a clear-cut lack of major goals is not conducive to self-fulfillment and can lead to an unsatisfactory life-style. If this type of generalized planning were used by a business, the results would be disastrous.

In the context of this book, the setting of major goals is essential to fulfillment because goals provide a basis for further action and the establishment of what really is and is not important. They should provide a foundation for living as solid as poured concrete.

The basic purpose of a life plan is to enable the selection of goals which are the most meaningful and which enable man to arrive at an order of priority which maximizes his life. A well-designed plan provides a frame of reference which avoids the trap of having a specific goal assume a value beyond its worth. For example, the man who permits his quest for money or power to result in the neglect of his family or his health has obviously done a poor job of setting major goals. On the other hand, if a man's work is neglected because of his outside interests, his plans have also failed. Realistically, however, excellence in a job can flourish when a man sees his goals in their true perspective and when he seeks to realize and fulfill himself.

The process of realizing potential provides a frame of reference for life planning which is both comprehensive and practical. The following exercise will enable the reader to personally apply to his own special situation the components developed in this book. It will develop the desire to define goals clearly and to make them realistic and challenging.

One of the important problems in life planning often lies in arriving at a central purpose for one's life. As set forth in Chapter 2, realizing one's own unique potential to live fully is the purpose and the theme of this book, and each component is related to that purpose.

Exercise—Specification of the Life Plan

On a blank sheet of paper write at the top *Realizing My Own Unique Potential to Live Fully.* General and important goals such as happiness, success, and peace of mind are encompassed within this heading. They are important to living fully and are a result of following through on more specific goals.

Next list the following columns: at the far left, *Vertical Potential;* along the same line over to the right, *Horizontal Potential.* Under *Horizontal Potential,* list these subheads: family, health, contributory, and cultural, recreational, and social. Bear in mind that writing down major goals crystallizes muddled thinking and will enable you to analyze, consider, refine, and update your goals individually and in relationship to each other. At this point, your paper should look like this:

REALIZING MY OWN UNIQUE POTENTIAL TO LIVE FULLY
Happiness——Success——Peace of Mind

VERTICAL POTENTIAL	HORIZONTAL POTENTIAL			
	Family	Health	Contributory	Recreational Cultural, Social

In the context of realizing potential, certain goals are common selections and would appear on any list of goals. The first of these preset goals should be listed under the column *Vertical Potential.* This goal would be *Development and Maintenance of Vertical Competence.* It was suggested previously that the development of vertical competence requires a minimum achievement level of 7, and therefore this goal would not be optional. Under this heading you would then list the vertical goals which are important to you. For example, a man might want to be promoted to a new position, or make $25,000 a year, or sell $1 million of his product a year, or improve his technical skills.

You will observe as you complete your life plan that many of your goals require money: for education, a new home, taking a trip, or retirement, to list only a few. Of course money requires vertical competence. Life goals will point up the relationship and importance of money to a particular life-style. The more goals require money, the more clearly one must evaluate all of his goals. Clear judgment and compromise are required in this vital area.

Because of the need for an adequate income and the fact that a great portion of a businessman's time is spent at his work, the full use of vertical potential is necessary because, as mentioned before, it spills over into other areas of life and permeates them. It relates to, and has impact on, other goal areas listed on your sheet.

At this point, under the *family* heading, write "a strong and loving family relationship." If this is not a permanent goal, a man has a problem. Write down your goals under this heading. As with all goals, each decade of life will vary. For example, a man age 35 might list under this heading: "to buy a new home"; "to build educational funds"; "to rent a place at the seashore for a month in the summer." A man at age 55 might have none of these particular goals.

In the case of the younger man especially, there will ordinarily be a strong correlation between family goals and vertical competence. Inflation makes rearing and educating children an expensive task. Other goals will also affect basic family goals; for example, recreational and social activities may or may not include the family, and the state of a man's health may affect his marital relations.

Under the *health* column, you should list another preset goal, *maintenance of physical fitness*. Every man should make this a major goal. You then list your own goals, such as losing weight, exercising, quitting smoking, or cutting down on drinking, or whatever is important to you. Physical fitness relates in one way or another to every goal you set, and it should occupy a prominent place in your life planning. Doctor William R. Barclay, chairman of the American Medical Association Committee on Hypertension, said recently, "The maintenance of health has a low priority in this country; it's only when you get sick that you put a high priority on health, on getting well. If we could change people's habits, we'd make a tremendous impact."

The remaining headings have no preset goals. Whether a man wishes to fish, swim, go to the opera, work with the Boy Scouts, study the piano, enjoy photography, or engage in one of a hundred other activities is a personal judgment. These goals are an important part of life and provide balance and enjoyment. They also relate to other goals in the allocation of one's time.

At this point, evaluate your list!

1. First, is the goal realistic for you? For example, certain goals may require a high level of intelligence of training, or the ability to respond favorably to lots of pressure, or a high level of physical stamina. Do you have the necessary characteristics and requisites or desire to achieve that goal? Cross out those goals that are not realistic.

2. Do you want to be a vertical achiever at a level of 7, or is your drive and ambition such that you should seek an 8 or 9? The nature of your goals can indicate which path is right for you. The older man may well ask, "Am I maintaining my competence in my work?"

3. Under each heading, number your goals from 1 to 10 on the basis of their importance. Here you are trying to arrive at priorities. As you develop your life plan, you begin to eliminate and cross off low-priority items. Your final list should be streamlined and flexible. By eliminating low-priority items, you eliminate conflicts between goals and thus greatly simplify life.

4. Your life plan should be reviewed and refined until you arrive at a program that has been looked at on several different occasions. You will find that each time you review your plan sheet you will have some different answers and some different perspectives about your goals. As the quality of your life improves, so will your life-plan sheet, and it will also reflect different goals for the different decades of your life.

Putting Goals into Action

With the suggested guidelines you should find it quite easy to prepare your own life plan. It should be a document designed to provide balance in your life and should enable you to set standards against which you can measure your activities and progress. It should be at all times a flexible, creative document. The idea, of course, is that *you* run it—it doesn't run you.

After such a list has been prepared, begin to implement your most important goals by listing the activities you intend to do in order to accomplish a specific goal.

Exercise—Choosing Priorities

Take a fresh sheet of paper and write one of your major goals at the top of it. Under it, list all the activities that you feel might enable you to constructively meet this goal. For example, assume that your goal is to cut down on weight. You might list some of the following: no desserts; reduce intake of carbohydrates; skim milk instead of whole milk; no candy; a thirty-minute walk every day; arrive at the ideal weight; check weight every morning on the scale; cut down the size of food portions. The activities you list provide the means for accomplishing your goal.

Next, classify the various activities in order of importance, numbering from 1 through 10. The creative job having been done, it's time to begin to set priorities and to eliminate particular activities. This list should be slashed and pruned at will. The idea is to consciously think through a priority schedule of activities so that the mind can go to work on what is really important to you and come up with creative thought.

Extrinsic and Intrinsic Goals

All goals should maximize the rewards for their achievement. This payoff can be external, in the form of money, recognition, prestige, etc., or internal, in a strong feeling of self-respect, self-esteem, a feeling of competence, and a sense of winning. There is much discussion in life about money, possession, power, etc., and little about the intrinsic satisfactions.

Exercise—Deciding on Satisfactory Rewards

For this step you need four activity sheets, one each for vertical, family, health, and other goals which represent your most important objectives.

In striving for vertical potential a man will seek a fair money return for his efforts, and through pride and competence in his work he can boost his self-image and the winning feeling, which are so important to his well-being. His goals therefore should be carefully structured to maximize both intrinsic and extrinsic rewards. For example, if an activity in his work produces stress, he should find a way around it to an activity that leads instead to a winning feeling.

The rewards of family goals in the form of love and the satisfaction a parent gets when a child does well in life are examples of a high form of intrinsic reward. The maintenance of physical fitness contributes in a major way to self-confidence and self-respect. Externally, a man will also look better when he is fit. If one chooses to play tennis for physical fitness and if it proves to be frustrating because of its competitive nature, forget it and find an exercise such as walking, swimming, riding a bike, or any activity that is enjoyable.

The same test should be applied to other activities so that they are enjoyable and contribute to the sense of well-being. Cross out those activities which are marginal.

Exercise—Consolidating and Finalizing

The final step is to take a single sheet of paper and list only the very top priority activities from all other sheets. You will have a pruned down, realistic, and hard-hitting life plan which has considered every facet of your life.

Recently, several men have mentioned to me that their fathers had said shortly before they died that their life had been a failure. One must wonder whether these men had a strong, vital life plan or if they (more likely) lacked a program to realize their own unique potential. Let's consider the three basic components of goal structuring: the rules for goal setting, building meaning into the system, and goals and giving.

Component 1 — The Rules for Goal Setting

While setting business goals is a very sophisticated and individual procedure, certain basic principles are common to both business and personal goals. These principles are fundamental to realizing potential and enabling a man to make goals his own. They have a marked relationship to a man's ability to use visualization as a tool in his growth.

Goals Should Be Clearly Defined

At a meeting some years ago I remember that the speaker asked his audience to hold their breaths as long as they could, and he timed them. After this was done, he said to the group, "Look at your watches, and hold your breath for three minutes." With a clear objective in mind, the group held their breaths far longer than they did on the first try. The point, of course, is that the more clearly we define the target, the greater the opportunity we have to move successfully toward the goal. Goals that are clearly defined should be measurable and should be accomplishable within a specific period of time.

An example of a goal that is poorly defined is in the following statement: "I want to earn a good living." This goal is too broadly stated. What is meant by the term "good living"? How much income do you need, and in what period of time? How will your expenses relate to the income you want to earn? In what period of time do you wish to earn this so-called good living? Contrast this with the goal, "I expect to be earning $25,000 a year by the end of next year." This goal is definite and sets a time limit for its achievement. In other words, there is a specific target to shoot at and a specific period of time for the achievement of the goal. It precipitates the planning necessary to achieve it and prescribes time for the achievement of the goal. The results and the progress toward it can be easily measured. On the other hand, indefinite and vague goals can prove frustrating to the point where they affect our self-confidence, increase our response to pressure, and disrupt the entire process of realizing potential. The more clearly the goal is defined, the quicker the mechanical parts of our minds will direct us toward its achievement.

It is not possible to overemphasize the desirability of goals that are a man's own and not somebody else's, and which are defined with great clarity. This clarity of thought builds direction into the system and causes the mind to seek the ways to achieve the goal. When we define a goal precisely, we begin to dwell on its image, we become enthusiastic, and we develop the desire to achieve it. Through visualizing and repeating a clear goal, it becomes so real that all of the powerful forces of the mind and body are called into play. What is at first only a possibility turns into a probability. These favorable results cannot happen if we are dealing in generalities. For example, if we say that we want to have a great year, or set a fabulous record in a particular area, or develop the greatest skill, we are not defining a goal and the lack of specifics reduces our efficiency because we are spread too thin. In addition to clarity, there is another essential element in setting goals.

Goals Should be Challenging and Realistic

To be fully effective, goals should enable a man to grow, but without negative stress. They should therefore be based on a true assessment of the individual's situation and on his development, abilities, and circumstances at a given time. The goal "I want to earn $25,000 a year by the end of next year" may or may not be realistic. If a man is making $10,000 a year now, it may not be realistic to expect him to jump to $25,000. On the other hand, if he is earning $20,000 a year now, a

$5,000 growth may well be realistic and challenging. If a goal is realistic and challenging, a man will feel that he has a reasonable chance to achieve the particular goal. Many writers on this subject feel that an individual should have a fifty-fifty chance of achieving a particular goal, which is to say that a goal can be on the upward side but should be within reason. To make a goal challenging and realistic, we should not let goals run us. The objective is to use goals so that we are in control. If goals are not realistic, they can be very negative and discouraging, and one of the most common stumbling blocks of goal setting is fear of failure.

Have you noticed how comfortable it is to work within present performance limits? The term "comfort zone" has been used to define these limits, and the term is very descriptive. To set goals beyond a comfort level of performance takes courage and effort. How much easier it is to stay at a low level, to be comfortable, to avoid the risks and failures that go with challenge and growth. But the man who would motivate himself avoids the mediocrity trap because he seeks the extrinsic and intrinsic rewards that follow the development of his potential. He gladly risks failure in exchange for the opportunity of success.

Goals not clearly defined and unrealistic can be an important factor in the development of stress and a negative response to pressure. Perhaps the most important objective discussed in this book is the development of a positive response to pressure. In the context of realizing our own unique potential, we're trying to make goal structuring work for us and not against us. We want to move ahead, to grow, to continuously realize our potential, but we want to do it in a way that's fun.

Because of the sophistication of goal setting today, it is not necessary here to belabor the need for setting challenging goals. In the presence of stress, however, both the underachiever and the overachiever can produce a negative response to pressure, since one wants too little, the other too much. The development of realistic, challenging, and nonstressful goals is a highly personal matter, and is related in one way or another to all of the components of process.

Isolating Problems and Getting Help

In setting goals we need to isolate and identify the problems which stand in the way of our goals. Some of these problems we will have to solve; others we will simply have to avoid. These problems may be personal in nature. They may relate to the fact that we are afraid to fail, or that we can't clearly define goals, or that we will not accept challenging and realistic goals. They may have to do with the ability of the man to manage his own time or with avoidance of the leveling-out process. Or, there may be problems in the way of the goals which relate to the business having to do with the economy, or competition, or the fact that we are not organized, or perhaps a feeling that our boss is not doing for us what we think he should be doing. The objective is to identify the key problems and then to determine in a realistic way how we're going to handle them.

There is a marked relationship of other people to our own goal setting. Those who set positive goals seek all the help they can get. It is a fact that a creative man can profit enormously if he is associated with others with whom he is in harmony. Such a relationship secures for him the complete benefit of the experience, training, education, specialized knowledge, and ability of others, just as completely as if their minds were his own. The key to this lies in the phrase "The Harmonious Coordination of Effort." The man who is realizing potential knows that he needs to draw on the strength of others, and that this is a normal part of his taking personal charge. He therefore associates with others who are willing and able to be of assistance to him in the pursuits of his personal goals. He tactfully avoids those who are negative, and he seeks to encourage his own positive outlook through his relationship to his associates and to others. The man dedicated to growth has positive friends, in the same way he has positive goals. His aim is to draw upon the unusual capacities of men so that he can adopt the best of their characteristics to assist him in reaching his goals.

Goals Must Have Balance

We cannot do everything in life. For example, all men are limited by the amount of time available, and most men are limited by the amount of money they can spend on their goals. It becomes necessary, therefore, to select those goals which are the most fulfilling. In the process of realizing potential, the selection of balanced goals is an individual judgment, but there are some ground rules:

1. The selection should involve consideration of the mental, physical, and spiritual dimensions of life. This is developed later in Chapter 6 as the whole-man concept.

2. A man's pursuit of his vertical potential can have a marked effect on his goals. For example, those who seek to excel in their work often have limited time to devote to outside affairs, yet the achiever usually finds balance through his family and recreational pursuits. On the other hand, a very high vertical index becomes detrimental if it damages a man's health and family life because of his search for money and power or because of a compulsive pursuit of excellence.

3. Horizontal development (which basically consists of the activities involving the family, and recreational, cultural, social, and community pursuits) is productive if it is fulfilling and satisfying. In vertical achievement at a level of 7, it's the individual's choice as to the blend of vertical and horizontal competence. No man has the right to be smug about his particular selection, for what fulfills one individual may not fulfill another.

Component 2 — Building Meaning into the System

The second component of goal structuring relates to building the meaning of the goal into the system so as to maximize the chances for its achievement. The process here is somewhat like what happens to us when we hear a steak sizzling and smell the burning charcoal. Our whole system can be activated toward the goal of eating the steak. This occurs because we are motivated to a marked degree by what our goals mean to us, by the sizzle we hear. The realization of potential is greatly dependent on the meaning of our goal to us, for lukewarm goals do not adequately develop the positive mind, faith in ourselves, purpose, or response to pressure.

The man who has no real interest in a particular goal has a problem, and if the goal is an important one, such as his work, his entire life may be affected adversely. The more deeply a man feels his goals, the more they become part of his bloodstream, the quicker he will move toward their achievement. Men who are experts in human behavior constantly discuss the need for meaningful goals for people generally. People function best when their goals are important to them and to others.

Consider the situation of an average businessman whose work is becoming more complex each year. What was once a relatively simple task now requires effort and study to keep up to date technically. He is apt to be strongly affected by economic forces beyond his control as business responds to increasingly powerful factors affecting supply and demand. Inflation, with its affect on employees' purchasing power, puts great pressure on the expenses of his division or business. At the same time, the goals he must meet become more difficult and more stressful as management pressures increase, and finally, as his income increases, so does the creativity of his job increase—and his problems. This portrait is presented not to engender sympathy for the businessman but to point up the fact that unless a man is growing, events will pass him by. A most vital impetus to this growth is his conviction that his goals are important and meaningful.

Visualization

Perhaps the most significant method of developing the meaning of goals is through the art of visualization. It was pointed out previously that cybernetic studies show that our minds do not differentiate between a real and an imaginary experience. It's not necessarily what you see—it's what you believe you see. If you think you see a bear, you will be just as frightened as if you actually saw one. In our minds we define the picture of a goal and the mind acts on that picture automatically and impersonally. Through visualization we are able to practice and develop our goal images, whether that goal is to improve our golf swing, to make more income, or to be more productive. The fact that we move automatically and without conscious effort toward our goal images emphasizes the need to visualize goals in a positive way. The ability to imagine and to deeply feel what it would be like to achieve a goal will accelerate progress toward the goal by building meaning into the system.

A major key to the realization of potential depends on an individual's ability to produce clear mental images or pictures. This is similar to the need to see the road ahead clearly when driving an automobile. Everyone has had the experience of being enveloped in a fog on the road. You immediately slow down and, if the fog is bad enough, you stop. The point is that one will act hesitantly and without confidence if the road ahead is not clear. As soon as the fog lifts and you can see the road again, you will proceed with confidence and certainty to your destination.

The reason for using visualization is that it clears away the mental fog which can obscure one's daily activities. When a man is preoccupied and not fully aware of what is going on around him, he is unable to form a clear picture of the action he should take. Until such time as he sees clearly the path he should follow, his actions will be slow and hesitant. A salesman who is preoccupied and who does not fully comprehend what the prospect is saying, or an employee who does not understand what the boss is trying to tell him, can waste weeks of time and sometimes destroy a sale or a relationship that has taken months to create.

The ability of an individual to keep pace with the rapid rate of technological change, to maintain productivity, and to remain emotionally well balanced will increasingly depend on his ability to develop new and better mental pictures of his current plans and his goals. To act effectively, he must sharpen his view of the changing situations he faces. Yet in many people, preoccupation and lack of awareness are commonplace.

The following classic example illustrates the development of preoccupation and its impact.

Jim Jones of the ABC Corporation was one of the brightest college graduates the corporation had ever recruited. His grades in school had been excellent, he had worked during the summer, and he had clearly shown great promise. The ABC Corporation placed Jim in its sales department to give him experience in this valuable area of the business. Jim embarked on his new career with tremendous enthusiasm. He began to do a creditable job of salesmanship. In the meantime he married, and within the next two years had his first child. He became increasingly interested in activities outside of work, such as tennis, reading the current magazines, tending the garden, and taking care of the baby, to name but a few of his extracurricular activities.

At this point, Jim was transferred into the production department at the Home Office. He found himself with a boss who seemed stern and uncompromising, and who was regarded as a difficult man. Jim had difficulty communicating with him. As the years rolled along in this job, Jim bought a new house, expanded his standard of living to a high level, and began to depend on his year-end bonus to keep solvent. As his stake in his company's benefits increased, he became less interested in voicing his concerns when things really became frustrating. Because he was so skilled in his job, he could think of other things, of his family, of his home, of his sports, when trouble developed. He began to lose interest in keeping up to date technically, and he increasingly lost zest for his job.

When the ABC Corporation became involved with a government contract requiring new equipment, new lines, and new technical information, Jim found himself literally unable to keep up with the situation. He had become a victim of stereotyped, repetitive behavior and had lost control of himself. He had become dependent on others and his environment for his support. Through the years he had become increasingly preoccupied and less able to cope with change in his work. He had ceased to have a clear picture of who he was and what his goals were. He was no longer aware of his own role in the changing circumstances. As a result, when an important job opened up, a younger man was given the appointment that Jim had so much wanted.

If we have a goal which is clearly defined, which is realistic and challenging, we then have an opportunity to picture what it would be like to achieve this goal and be active in it. We can, through our thoughts, become enthusiastic about it. We have the opportunity to dwell upon the goal and to arouse a deep desire for it. Through repeated emphasis on a specific, well-defined goal, the mind begins automatically to set the course toward the goal and to compensate when we get off course.

For example, suppose a goal is to develop one's self-confidence in speaking before people, and to learn to regard that experience as a very desirable one.

Exercise — Visualization

The technique of visualization might be as follows:

Close your eyes and feel a euphoric relaxation descending through your body. Start counting down from 10 to 0, feeling more deeply relaxed with each step. When you reach zero, imagine that you're on a stage about to talk. The curtains are closed, and you can hear the audience quieting down. When the curtains open, you see yourself standing behind the lectern, poised and ready to speak. You see yourself as being totally self-confident, relaxed and outgoing, yet formal. The microphone is on the lectern and you use it to speak to your audience. A glass of water is on your left side. Your notes are on the lectern, but you really do not need them. You can visualize them and you turn them as you speak, but they are not really necessary because of the thoroughness with which you know your subject. While you're talking, you see faces in the audience displaying interest and warmth. You see yourself pause in your talk to take a drink of water. You hear your voice. It is clear, strong, perfectly modulated, and expressing your thoughts clearly and without strain. You feel as if you were talking to an intimate group of your friends in your own home, and you know that you are doing your job in a first-rate fashion. You feel totally at ease and in harmony with your surroundings and with the audience.

If this exercise is used each day for a period of a week or two, the fear of speaking should leave and it can turn out to be a thoroughly enjoyable experience. Again the visualization of this experience should be as vivid as one can possibly make it. An interesting experiment is to have someone read the above exercise to you while you mentally live the experience.

In developing further the ability to visualize, the following exercise can be valuable.

Exercise — Visualizing Congenial Surroundings

Assume that the goal is to create a retreat in one's mind where a man can pause to catch his breath. You see a room where one can mentally retire to rest and be completely free of stress, and where one can feel completely at home:

First, feel yourself becoming increasingly relaxed; breathe regularly and deeply and begin the count from 10 to 0. As you feel yourself becoming more and more relaxed, project on your mental viewing screen a small, comfortable room where you feel totally safe and secure. Whenever you enter this room, all fears and apprehensions will leave. As you shut the door, you hear the latch snap into place.

The room itself, small and comfortably furnished, contains your favorite chair. The room is carpeted so that you walk comfortably and soundlessly. The carpeting and the drapes shut out the noise of the outside world and the drapes allow a soft light to enter the room. You have a feeling of freedom and relaxation, and cares do not intrude upon the serenity in this room.

You visualize on your imaginary screen a fireplace and other comfortable furnishings. You see yourself retreating to this room, where you can think out effortlessly and calmly any problem and for which, inevitably, the solution will be forthcoming. As you practice visualizing this mental retreat, your mind will turn naturally and normally to it for periodic rest. If things get too intense, the image of this haven can be a valuable relaxation technique.

There are innumerable methods of using visualization to achieve goals, whether the goal is to lose weight, to relax, to stop smoking, or to develop specific business goals. Through visualization a man can develop any component in each checkpoint in the process of realizing his potential. Visualization is, in a sense, *creative* daydreaming, during which time a person may program his mind in a positive way and utilize the remarkable powers of his mind.

A simple practice exercise, from a business standpoint, would be to decide what you would like to be doing in a specific area a year hence. Then begin to imagine, in detail, what it might feel like if you were to achieve this particular goal. Visualize the obstacles you have overcome as well as your successes, and think of the people who might be associated with you in this imaginary successful effort. Use the mental viewing screen in your mind to develop and embellish and to bring alive what this successful achievement would be like.

Demand Performance

A longtime friend, who is now the president of one of the largest corporations in America, has often discussed his philosophy of demand performance with me. Simply stated, his goals are always on the up side, they are challenging and realistic, and they demand that he perform within nonstressful limits. In essence, he is able to motivate himself. He conveys in crystal-clear terms to the men who work for him that he expects them to utilize their abilities. He does not demand that a man do more than he is capable of, but no one works for him without moving in the direction of realizing his potential. He has been responsible for the growth of many men.

Industry is growing increasingly expert in delineating demand performance for their creative people by means of a set of extraordinarily clear objectives, with a close follow-up of results by others, which demands performance of the individual.

The leader of men has, to a greater degree than most men, the ability to motivate himself. Early in his career, the self-motivator is able to do more than accept the goals of others. He has the capacity to challenge himself and to structure goals in such a way that he forces himself to do the difficult jobs. Rather than trying to maintain the status quo, his goals remain challenging and demanding and force him to greater achievement. Because of his dedication to growth, he builds meaning into his system by setting challenging objectives that lead him to do the more difficult jobs. Demand performance applied to others by men who expect much from themselves can help a man to grow to the point where his main thrust comes from within himself, which is the best place. I have observed many men reach high levels of performance through imposing on themselves high-level standards of performance.

Everyone knows what it takes to warm up to a task, either physically or mentally; if we are forced to continue forward, our fatigue increases up to a certain point and then gradually diminishes, and we are fresher than before. This appears to be a new level of energy, the "second wind." Ordinarily, we make no attempt to find that level because we are inclined to stop an activity as soon as the element of fatigue sets in. It is becoming increasingly apparent that this new level of energy can provide amounts of power that were never dreamed of. The individual who reaches this new level of energy does not wreck himself, for his body adjusts to the activity, and if he observes basic health rules, he needs no more rest than a person who is idle, if as much.

A very potent method, therefore, of building the meaning of goals into the system is that we demand our own performance and don't quit too soon, thus banking the furnace prematurely and therefore not permitting energy to develop fully. The man who is not banking the furnace is continuously upgrading his goals, within the limits of his capabilities at a particular time, until a level of performance is reached beyond which a balanced life cannot be maintained. Where demand performance is used, goals are so compelling that it is virtually impossible to level out. The desire for recognition, both financially and psychologically, is so great with some men that they literally panic when their goals are not being realized. They are very aware that they can go downhill as fast as they came up and that achievement is not a level road.

Very early in his career the man who is a self-motivator elects to set and master those goals which are for him the most difficult and for which the financial and emotional rewards are the greatest. He structures his goals carefully, and during a given day he will think about them many times. His goals are specific, and he concentrates on them so deeply during his working hours that they absorb him. He tends to operate free of harmful tension, and is intensely committed to his goals. He subscribes to the philosophy that excellence in his work is one of his major life objectives and that nothing can be more helpful than finding outlets for his time and energy in his chosen field. He has great drive to utilize his vertical potential, and this is important and has in itself great meaning to him.

In demand performance we also build the meaning of goals when we follow our progress closely. The more clearly and specifically we observe the results of our work, the easier it becomes to determine if our work is realistic and challenging. We learn from experience to enjoy the feelings of success and not to feel badly if occasionally we need to revise a goal downward.

In essence, we build meaning through all of the steps in

setting goals and through observing our progress. The more we demand this of ourselves, the faster we tend to reach our goals.

Management by Objectives

In recent years corporations have instituted a forcing system—management by objectives (MBO)—which is essentially a contract with your boss as to what you and he want the results of your efforts to be. There is detailed agreement on goals, quotas, performance standards, and a host of other items. In effect, your boss says, "Now I want you to do what you have to do to achieve these goals." The basis for the successful functioning of MBO is that it must be regarded as an action document, subject to feedback, corrective action, and new ideas.

The basic concept of MBO is unchallengeable. It is characteristic of most men that they are motivated by forces outside themselves. Management by objective provides a framework of expectation and a report card for a man's results. It can serve a much needed motivational purpose. The most forceful exponent of MBO to whom I talked put it this way: "Nothing can be more rewarding to anyone than to have a clear set of objectives and to have their performance measured as to whether or not they achieve their objectives. If properly structured this has the greatest single impact on potential. You set corporate objectives and you plan at every level. The man participates and assists in setting the standards. People developing plans will be more demanding of themselves."

Consider some comments from other men. One manager said: "I didn't like it at first but it gets everyone planning and nothing happens until people plan. In the food industry they call it 'management by mushroom.' You keep everyone in the dark and throw a little verbal horse manure around once in a while."

A district manager for a large corporation said, "There is a tendency for big business to be run by Harvard business graduates who really have not had extensive practical experience, who are not particularly sensitive to people, and who are trying to formalize their background as financial rather than being people-oriented. Because of this they have an insensitivity to people and a total dedication to the dollar sign and immediate profits. They're working with balance sheets, financial statements, and figures rather than with people."

A middle-management man said, "The contract is between you and your boss, but the problem is that the weight is all on one side. You really don't have a choice—it can't be equitable and there is a monumental amount of paperwork."

The truth of the matter is that while MBO can be unbelievably important in the development of potential, in the hands of an amateur it can become a detailed bookkeeping exercise which in the long run can inhibit potential. The amateur oversimplifies the job because of his inexperience. His theme is based on numbers in one form or another. He has no conception of the nuances, judgment calls, and feelings which have got to be considered. The simplistic manager thinks that numbers are all there are, and that's wrong.

MBO can build discipline and individual achievement to a high level if properly used. It functions best when there is a mutuality of interest in making the contract. It fails when an unspoken adversary position is created. It succeeds brilliantly when it is based on developing the subordinate's potential. Its long-term success is questionable if it is motivated solely by the "last year plus 10 percent" objective. It can bring out the best in a man if his boss is himself in the process of realizing his own potential. It will usually fail if the boss scores low in his own vertical potential.

To fully develop a man's long-term productivity (potential), MBO should be spiritual in origin. In this context it is perhaps one of the highest forms of "loving thy neighbor," for it implies that the boss desires to serve and to help the man who must execute the objective. It is based on the integrity, the self-respect, and the capacity of a man and not on figures ground out by an impersonal corporate entity. Such a concept does not alter the need for profit nor does it minimize the difficulties of reaching specific goals. What it does do is motivate a man to really want to reach and to exceed his objectives.

Component 3—Goals and Giving

The philosophy of giving has been referred to several times in this book. Is this an abstract concept, peculiar to the great religions of the world, or can it also be a philosophy of doing business? Erich Fromm, in his book *The Art of Loving*, has this to say about giving:

In the sphere of material things, giving means being rich. Not he who has much is rich, but he who gives much. . . . The most important spirit of giving, however, is not that of material things, but lies specifically in the human realm. What does one person give to another? He gives of himself, of the most precious he has, he gives of his life. This does not necessarily mean that he sacrifices his life for another — but that he gives him that which is alive in him; he gives of his joy, of his interest, of his understanding, of his knowledge, of his humor, of his sadness — of all expressions and manifestations of that which is alive in him. In thus giving of his life, he enriches the other person, he enhances the other's sense of aliveness by enhancing his own sense of aliveness. He does not give in order to receive; giving is in itself exquisite joy, but in giving he cannot help bringing something to life in the other person, and this which is brought to life reflects back to him; in truly giving he cannot help receiving that which is given back to him.*

In a business context, the art of giving is an integral part of realizing potential. In business, giving cannot be expected to be in the form of services for which no pay is received. Businessmen expect to pay fairly those who work for them. By the same token, they expect to receive services in return that are worth the payment. There are those in the business world who seek their own gain even at the expense of others, or those

* Harper & Row, 1956, p. 24.

who are governed by the philosophy of quid pro quo, where nothing more is ever given than is necessary to be reasonable and fair.

In the context of the process of developing potential, however, the act of giving is represented by the willingness of a man to give more of himself than he is obligated to do for those whom he serves. The ability to give in business implies a willingness on the part of a man to go the extra mile for his employer or his customer. He gives more of himself than is required—in his effort, his interest, enthusiasm, skill, and time.

Highly creative men often have a deep commitment to spiritual or philosophic ways which serve mankind, and their values are expressed through their goals and their life's work. Their energy, alertness, and love of life make them the envy of those around them. Their dedication affects all strata of their lives, and the more intense their dedication the more they seem to function at their maximum output.

The goal of giving activates the qualities of the positive mind. It materially enhances the opportunity for vertical growth in business, for a giving attitude is easily recognized by an employer. It also enhances the intrinsic assets of self-respect and a feeling of usefulness and competence. The art of giving freely of one's self in business, without regard for personal compensation, is a powerful tool in the process of realizing potential.

Skills and Giving

The person who generates creative activities in his work is constantly sharpening his abilities to manage or to sell. In a business context, developing work skills makes it possible to give freely of one's self. For example, when a salesman develops momentum, almost everything he does seems to come more easily. His belief in himself and his work is at a peak. In the area of management skills, he tends to increase his competence in goal setting and time management. In the service and sales area, his understanding and knowledge of his product also develop for the benefit of his customers.

In essence, as the components developed in this book integrate, they tend to produce a higher level of skills through more study, the better use of time, and the sheer impact of momentum. A man becomes a giver.

Summary

The person who develops goal structuring as an art adds the quality of excitement to his life, for it is exciting to have positive, challenging goals, and it is about the best possible prescription for boredom and frustration. Once a strong goal is put into the mind, it acts like a magnet which draws upon all of the resources of an individual. This magnetizing action is indicative of the basic principle by which our thoughts align with their physical equivalent; or, stated differently, our thoughts translate themselves into reality.

Through goal setting we have the opportunity to chart the course by which to steer our lives, rather than to be tossed about like flotsam on the sea. A vital and indispensable part of growth for any person lies in striving toward meaningful goals, with the full knowledge that as they are approached, new goals must be set. The person always in process never arrives; his fun and satisfaction come primarily from the struggle for the goal and not the achievement of it. We use goals to create a road map for our own use; we are not letting goals take charge of us. Goal setting involves having the courage and confidence to try new things, and to discard the old because of the interest and excitement in a new challenge. In a sense you substitute something better for something which has served its purpose.

We can be reminded of the basic rules of setting goals by the key sentence "structured goals chart my course," which means that a goal should be clearly defined, realistic, and challenging. It also implies a strong element of control over one's life and implies that our goals should be our own and not somebody else's.

The meaning of our goals takes on a new dimension when goal setting is tied in with the purpose of realizing potential. At this stage, specific goals do not stand alone. A businessman, therefore, depends not only on the strength of his goals, but also on the depth of his purpose for growth, which can make the task of goal setting easier and more enjoyable. Meaningful goals can also be built into the human system through demand performance, preferably self-imposed, and through

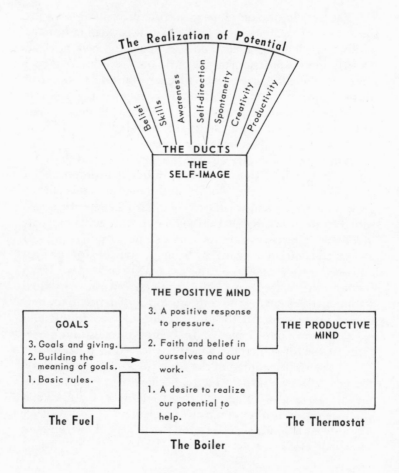

the ability to visualize and to experience in our minds a particular goal. Visualization is a major tool in setting goals.

The final ingredient is that of setting goals within a framework of giving and of maximizing our service to others. When this is achieved, the process of developing energy and intellect has become successful in an observable way. The effects of this development are presented by our self-esteem, our self-image, and our feelings of inner worth, which are manifested in the form of belief, skills, awareness, self-direction, spontaneity, creativity, and productivity. These characteristics are not accidental; they occur as a result of thought processes and actions which develop when a man engages in the process of realizing his potential.

The self-image and its overt expression are largely a result of the efficiency of goal setting and the activation of the positive mind. While our self-image is therefore a result of our prior actions, certain specific components of our self-esteem relate to growth. These are considered in Chapter 4.

4

Checkpoint 3 —
the self-image

The process of realization involves taking charge of our lives through the components of the positive mind and goal structuring, with the ultimate goal being an adequate and realistic self-image. A person must be able to look within himself and find a self that he is not ashamed of and that he can trust and believe in. This self-portrait is not a gift; it is an achievement and can represent progress that is sometimes painfully earned; it represents a running battle, a continued processing of ourselves, and unless we structure this picture carefully, feelings of inferiority and self-condemnation can be the brush we use on the canvas. An inadequate self-image is actually an opinion on our part; being an opinion, it can be changed, and it often involves beginning to draw a new portrait and to know and understand ourselves for what we truly are.

To progress vertically in his work, as well as to find life satisfying and rewarding, a person must develop a strong and favorable self-image. A recent study of a group of college students showed that 75 percent of them lacked confidence in themselves, and they suffered strongly from feelings of inferiority. Apparently this is a general tendency, for in the course of my daily meeting with businessmen in various levels of sales and management work, a rating of 5 or 6 was not uncommon. When we discussed the reason for their own low

rating, it often developed that its cause was not their compensation but in some lack of a full feeling of inner worth, of
self-esteem. It would appear that these negative feelings are
diluting the great capability of many men just enough so that
they have an adverse and detrimental effect. Yet these people
hold responsible positions and perform well in them.

The basis for our actions is rooted in the picture we hold of
ourselves, our relationships with others, and our environment.
This picture is our self-image, and everything we see or do will
correspond with it. If a man pictures himself as harassed and at
the mercy of forces beyond his control, he will act in accordance with this picture. On the other hand, a man who is
optimistic and who feels that he is in charge of himself will do
things which correspond with that image. The man who sees
himself in a certain way will begin to move in the direction of
that picture.

For example, I discussed the matter of potential with a
man, age 48, who ten years ago had left his career as an
orchestra leader to form a building corporation. In this time he
has created a large industrial park, a chain of motels, and a
complex of restaurants. The net worth of this company today
is approximately $12 million. With regard to his own potential
he said this: "I feel that I have been blessed with certain
God-given talents, and in terms of financial and business success I have been most fortunate. I think, however, that I have a
better potential for serving mankind through the political
process."

It developed as he talked that his political aspirations are at
a national level. Because he has reached a level of financial
success that few men achieve, his picture of himself has changed
from a money-oriented base to that of a life of true service. He
also said: "I believe that I have potential in this field because of
my business background and because I have no connection
with any form of political corruption." This man sees himself
in a new role, at a new level of horizontal competence; his goals
are beginning to change in accordance with that picture.

The Restricted Self-Concept

A restricted self-concept limits growth. If a man has a self-concept far below his real potential, he does not know himself. He loses the ability to see opportunities and to respond effectively to circumstances around him.

Quite frequently, the businessman who has settled for a mediocre performance is not at all mediocre. But, he adjusts to someone else's standards or to the belief that his security is his company's group and fringe-benefit programs. He plays it safe. He does what those around expect him to do, and he resists new ideas because they disturb him. He lives for the status quo and often dreams of the day he will retire. He puts the blinders on, and his self-image in his work becomes fixed, without creativity.

One of my good friends said to me recently, "You know, I have observed that mediocrity often starts at the top. My boss did a terrific job when he first took over. He really had everybody hopping, and over a seven-year period he had sales and profits up to a very high level. Then he reached a level that he felt was OK, and he began to relax—he sort of took retirement on the job. After a while the excitement left our company and our really aggressive men drifted away to other companies. The rest of us just kind of fitted in with the 'I've got it made' philosophy. We have a new president now, but he has a tough job on his hands."

A restricted self-image does not fully enable a person to share himself with others. (Who can love his neighbor when he does not love himself?) In the absence of love of self, self-esteem can become self-doubt, self-concern, and self-rejection. The negative feelings are created and embellished by how we think. If our attention is drawn to failure, we will feel insecure, and through the power of visualization we tend to create the very condition we fear.

For example, in sales work, men develop what is called the "hot doorknob" syndrome. A salesman can create an image of hostility in the minds of new customers on whom he should call. He can develop a fear of rejection, of receiving a no, to such a degree that he shrinks from opening a new door, of calling on a new account. He mentally withdraws from the new call as though the doorknob were literally hot. A similar thought process develops on a golf tour when the nerves of a fifty-year-old show on the short putts. He has missed enough of them to affect his image.

On the other hand, the man in the process of realizing his potential has an expanding self-concept, which is based primarily on self-understanding and action. His objective is his own growth, externally and intrinsically. He does not leave this task to chance. He develops a philosophy which looks to his growth in a positive way and which involves dedication to his calling, to his own cause. This image he has of himself evokes a desire to develop his goals and to identify his areas for personal growth. Through the structure of "process" he maintains his own program of meaningful development. He reaches out for the help of those around him, and his constructive influence can be a powerful factor in the development of others.

Self-Image and Response to Pressure

The self-image concept has an important effect on a man's ability to respond positively to pressure. Why is it that under virtually identical circumstances, one man collapses under pressure while another goes on to great heights? I recently discussed this with a friend of mine in Philadelphia who at one time played football for Princeton and who is today known for his wonderful use of potential. He said, "When I played football on Franklin Field in front of 50,00 people I didn't stay nervous very long. In fact, the opposite happened; the adrenalin flowed, I became elevated, I became capable of performance above and beyond what I thought possible. I sometimes wonder if this didn't start when I was a child, for my mother never missed an opportunity to tell me that I was a good person. I guess she just instilled in me the idea that I am good." This man has a strong self-image and scored himself a 9 on the potential scale. A philosophy based on a sense of direction, and a strong feeling of personal identity and self-knowledge, has provided him with a foundation to meet stress in a positive way. For many years I have observed him in the process of growth. He believes in himself and has a deep conviction of what he wants and feels. He has a strong and rewarding self-image, and I have never seen him react negatively to pressure.

Stated differently, we need a personal philosophy based on strong, positive, personal, and business goals which are challenging but realistic so that they don't in themselves induce anxiety; we need to surround these goals with a "giving" attitude. Meaningful goals that we feel deeply provide an image of what we ought to pursue and what to believe in. Such goals go a long way in enabling a man to operate positively and without anxiety. As his self-concept grows, his guideposts come from a maturation within rather than from the directives predominating his childhood or from the outward circumstances of his particular job.

Some Basic Thoughts about Self-Image

Each man, therefore, has in mind a detailed picture of himself; it is not necessarily what he really is, but what he imagines himself to be. This is his self-image and is his evaluation of himself and his own abilities, his own capacities, and his own estimate of his worth as a person.

It is generally accepted today that the self-image of an individual determines in large measure his capacity to function effectively; or, stated differently, the self-image of an individual determines the area of the possible in any given project. Thus, if a man thinks, for example, that he is a poor speaker, it is unlikely that he will deliver an effective speech; and if a man thinks he is a poor manager, it is unlikely that he will effectively motivate others. In different terms we might say, "As a man thinketh in his heart, so is he." What a man thinks of himself in any given area determines his effectiveness in that area, and the attempt to operate out of this effective range introduces tension in an individual's performance, whatever his profession or occupation.

Everyone has seen a playoff on the professional golf tour where the entire match rested on a two-foot putt, which was missed. This is a shot the golfer could make a thousand times under ordinary circumstances, but in this instance his self-confidence was shaken by the importance of the shot and by the introduction of tension. Suddenly his performance was that of a duffer. At that particular moment he thought poorly of his ability to make the putt, and he immediately limited his effectiveness and therefore his ability to make the shot.

In the same way the performance of a man is circumscribed by the image he holds of himself in his mind. If his self-image is such that he lacks confidence in his ability to accomplish his goals, or if he has settled for mediocre performance as a way of life, he limits his potential for growth. However, if he becomes aware of this, if the components of the process of realization have been developed, the energy released must begin to be felt in the individual's appraisal of his own worth. The effect of realizing that something is happening and that a stronger self-image is developing brings about what might be termed "natural elation." There is a joyousness in the release of energy as opposed to its being restrained. In many respects it is like a teakettle of water which, if it is corked up when heated, will explode; if the steam escapes, the kettle sings.

A man who engages in the process of realization inevitably begins to develop and enhance his self-image. In order, however, to maximize development of the self-image, it should in itself be structured as an individual entity. Our own individual, private picture of ourselves is a key to winning, for it determines the richness of our life and our success in our work and in our personal life. The exciting thing is that we determine in a major way the nature of this image. There are a few basic considerations which play an important part in self-image development.

Know Yourself

You have to begin to truly know yourself. There often seems to be a perverse resistance to the business of understanding one's self. Unless a man understands his motivations, it is quite likely that he will be motivated by external circumstances, and he is then in the rather typical position of being in a state of drift and at the mercy of forces he does not understand. Without self-assessment, it is unlikely that we will discover our potentials, and it becomes extremely difficult to develop a realistic and adequate self-image. There can be no better way to begin to know yourself than by making a commitment to begin to realize your potential in life. Once such a commitment is made, the mind will automatically begin to explore sources of that potential. One must at the same time take the risks involved in growth when he ventures into new areas. These risks can result in his being ignored, rejected, and sometimes maligned.

For or Against?

You have to decide whether you're for yourself or against yourself. It is quite easy to avoid deciding the answer to this question. As a result, an individual can live a life where he is constantly putting himself down rather than lifting himself up. The nature of life is such that there will always be pain and trouble and loss involved in it. It becomes especially important in structuring the self-image that a man makes a decision to capitalize and appreciate his own good qualities. The point is that we can find richness beyond imagining if we can learn to love and nurture ourselves.

It is important that we encourage ourselves, that we lift ourselves up. Unless we decide to be for ourselves, we can suffer from forces within us which are not relevant to our current situation and which relate to our early childhood, or to our conscience, or to a private estimate of ourselves which is incorrect. A realistic appraisal of one's self can reveal that one is better, more capable, more creative than he imagines, that there are those who love and honor him, and that he has done rather well—he has a home, a good job, and a good reputation. We have to begin to be consciously aware that we have these many blessings. Being thankful for our lives, our families, our food, our opportunity to work, our freedom to think and worship, our opportunity to develop physically, mentally, and spiritually, all are part of structuring an adequate self-image.

Our Goals

You have to meet your own internal commitments. At times in self-image structuring, we are caught in the middle. Sometimes we demand too much of ourselves and may demand perfection to the point where we can treat ourselves in a destructive manner. Actually, in our battle for self-discovery, it can help if we imagine that we will emerge as neither a genius nor a saint. Our goal is to respect and trust ourselves.

On the other hand, it is unwise to ignore what our consciences tell us to expect of ourselves. If we're going to let our work slide, we had better find out how we're going to feel about it. If there is a substantial price tag in the form of self-recrimination, it is probably better to go and do the job. The fact is that we have to continue to listen to ourselves, to monitor our own internal dialogues, for we can pay too big a price for not understanding what we are telling ourselves.

A Value Judgment

You have to recognize that your self-image is a value judgment based on truth, and that truth is what you are today, being neither more nor less than you are. The self-image is not only what you are now but also what you can be tomorrow and the next year, for a commitment to growth involves development of potential and therefore the growth in the self-image itself. As our self-image grows, our capacity to improve our performance in life grows with it. The self-image is therefore a determinant of our life-style and of our effectiveness to perform in any part of our lives because of the basic fact that we act, and feel, and perform in accordance with what we imagine to be true about ourselves and our environment. Our actions, therefore, are not determined by circumstances and things as they really are, but according to our own private image of what these things are. The process of realization gives us the opportunity to paint a picture of ourselves, one that fulfills us. No other single judgment about ourselves is more important to us or to those around us.

Transactional Analysis

The modern philosophy of transactional analysis sheds light on the self-image—the estimate we make of ourselves —and one of its most important tenets is that feelings of inferiority are literally built into the human system. It is pointed out that inferiority and the basis for neurotic behavior start early in childhood. In fact, this is the universal position of early childhood, and because of his size and helplessness the child inevitably considers himself inferior to the adult. This condition exists in every child no matter how loving the parents. It occurs not only because of the larger size of the parent as compared with that of the child, but also because societal processing requires that the child be disciplined.

Because of these influences the child comes out of his early years with the basic life position that, while you are OK, he is not OK. It has been further established by this type of analysis that individuals tend to stay in this position for their entire lifetime unless a conscious decision is made at some point by the individual that he is, in fact, OK. Each individual, there- fore, has fixed self-negation in his mind, high-fidelity mental tape recordings of inferiority or not-OK feelings, which are ready for instant replay unless superseded by later recordings of self-confidence.

Transactional analysis has become popular because there is truth to it and because people can understand it. For perhaps the first time, a person realizes that everyone has deep-seated feelings of inferiority and that many of our current actions occur as a result of early childhood training. It is revealing to become aware that our self-image is impaired at an early age and that, unless we consciously change this fact, we can suffer damaging feelings of inferiority throughout our lives. When a person says, in effect, "I know I'm OK and you're OK," then transactional analysis becomes a positive force in self-image development.

The Effects of Feeling Not-OK

Even the most successful businessman can feel not-OK from time to time. While he may ordinarily feel very OK about his work and his life, latent not-OK feelings can readily assert themselves.

For example, a sustained and sharp reduction in sales or profits caused by competitive pressures can make a man believe his self-doubts. A salesman is particularly vulnerable to the not-OK. His ego is nourished by the approval of others, and if he too often hears no and not often hears yes in the course of his work, he can cease to feel OK. The effect on his sales results can be disastrous. While there are innumerable business and personal circumstances that can cause not-OK feelings, it is essential that they not be permitted to persist for long periods of time. If not-OK feelings continue to develop, they interfere with the functioning of all the components covered in this book.

Because a positive mind is essential to increased productivity and success, it is clear that the first priority of a businessman is to learn to feel OK, closely followed by the ability to stay OK when the going gets rough. In terms of the process of realizing potential, being OK is not an accident. It is a result of a series of positive actions involving self-discipline and self-motivation, which provide a solid base for a strong self-image.

Three basic components of a strong self-image will be considered in the subsequent discussions: the self-image and the process, living with ourselves, and a new level of competence.

Component 1—The Self-Image and the Process

A major objective of the process of realizing potential is the development of a strong, continuing support system for the self-image. This is an undergirding for a realistic and adequate self-image which encourages a man to seek out his potential for growth and which can maintain it. Through examination of his own thought processes, his goals, and his attitudes toward himself and his job, he gains an ever-deepening self-understanding. Through the development of this self-knowledge, he becomes more aware of his aims, strengths, and weaknesses. He begins to take charge of becoming the kind of a person his potential indicates he should be.

The process of realizing potential develops the inner strength of a man. He becomes increasingly aware of who he is, where he wants to go, and what he wants to be. The development of a personal philosophy that is clearly defined enables a man to withstand the stress of change which inevitably comes. Through this foundation he gains the freedom to be his own man and to control his own destiny. Through his growth he develops a self-image which is based on truth, and recognizes his own inner worth rather than a self-concept which draws its strengths from the external recognitions of others and which collapses, like a house of cards, under stress.

A man might say at this point: "I see what you mean, and I intend to get a better picture of myself in this chosen work of mine. I'm going to be self-confident, strong, and effective." While this is a desirable goal, and can well be a starting point in enlarging a self-concept, it will not hold up to the hard facts of life unless he is a professional at what he is doing and has a strong support system for his work. For example, Eugene Ormandy, the well-known conductor of the Philadelphia Orchestra, is both an artist and a professional at leading the orchestra. He undoubtedly has a strong image of his confidence and ability to lead the orchestra, and this image is based on the fact that he is a talented professional who knows precisely what he is doing. He is well aware of the competence of the men who play under his direction, and he completely rehearses each program. This self-image is based on truth and is supported by a proven system.

There are many men who construct a support system for their lives which is based almost entirely on external factors —the trappings of power and prestige, money, and a certain job. If these supports are suddenly withdrawn, they face a major life crisis. In the stock-market crash of 1929, many committed suicide when their external support system collapsed. In the same manner, many of the crises of middle age are precipitated by values which are too shallow to last a lifetime.

In a businessman's case, these central values are based upon the components and the process of growth. As he learns to understand and enlarge his self-concept, he can more effectively control his behavior in setting realistic goals and in understanding those values which are of real importance to him.

If a man concludes that he wants to stand for something, if he wants to grow and improve, it's his responsibility and no one else's. He has to plan and take control of his activities in order to enlarge and expand his self-image.

In discussing process and the self-image with a group of men, the consensus of what everyone wanted seemed to be as follows: I realize that through engaging in the process of realizing my potential, I can begin to know more about myself, to improve my effectiveness in my work, and to develop my strengths. I realize that how I see myself affects my work, my emotions, and my growth. I can accept the components in this process as valid because they are checkpoints for my potential, to use as I alone see fit. I would expect to use process to develop and increase my external rewards in the form of income, savings, and recognition. But I am equally interested in the intrinsic rewards of an increasing self-esteem, a feeling of competence, and a sense of belonging. I want a philosophy of life which is clearly defined and which is strong enough to withstand the stress of life.

The process of realizing potential emphasizes internal searching for the truth about ourselves. Through self-awareness a man develops reserves of strength which are independent of external conditions and which are built on rock rather than the shifting sands of competitive business. Through process, his goals and his supports become his own and are not disciplines imposed by others.

This support system is grounded in giving of one's self, in commitment and dedication to personal growth, in the avid pursuit of the positive mind, and in powerful goals which are brilliantly defined and which belong to us. This provides the nucleus of a code of behavior, a basic frame of reference, from which a fulfilling self-concept can emerge, one that can withstand the test of time.

As the self-concept develops into a true picture, and as it grows and matures, a remarkable event occurs. Ever so subtly a man begins to change, to transcend himself. It is as though he has planted a crop in fertile ground, which is then watered, fertilized, and kept free of weeds and insects. Slowly but surely the seedlings begin to sprout and grow. In the early stages these sprouts are weak and tender and require special care, but as they develop they become strong.

And so it is with a man's growth. The seedlings he plants are those of enthusiasm, faith, courage, empathy, optimism, love, hope, and all of the positive responses which are so conducive to health, efficiency, and the good life. Through his commitment to the development of his own potential and the steps in the process, he magnetizes his condition and begins to use powers which belong to him but which have not been fully used. He has begun the ultimate search for self-fulfillment.

Component 2—Living with Ourselves

Ego Stroking

It is a recognized fact that infants have a great need to be physically touched and that they will not grow normally unless they are handled and fondled. This requirement gradually turns into a hunger for recognition itself as well as the need for physical stroking. The practice may involve a smile, a nod, a handshake, the art of listening attentively, or a statement of recognition by another person. Stroking should be done with integrity; it should square with the facts and not be overdone. It should be supported by feelings of good faith and goodwill on the part of both parties. The opposite of stroking is what can be termed put-down. For example, in business a manager may say to one of his men, "You're lying down on the job," or "Your results now indicate that you have a little too much money for your own good," or "You're wasting too much time with outside activities." These may be considered as put-downs. Contrast this with the case of a salesman, whose manager says, "Joe, you're tremendous. Over the last month you made twelve calls and had nine orders. Just imagine what would have happened had you made twenty-four calls." This kind of stroking sends a man away feeling good about his capacity and wondering what *might* happen if he were to make twenty-four calls in the following month.

The great managers of men are those who have learned how to stroke in a positive way. They avoid put-downs which may damage an individual's self-image and which provoke negative reactions. A great motivator of men is himself in the process of growing and is devoted to the cause of helping others to realize their potential. Being guided by the process of realization, he makes authentic and helpful comments, and recognizes that the man to whom he is talking is important. He freely expresses feelings of warmth and closeness; he has learned to reveal more of himself by eliminating false masks and substitutes from his own life.

The ability to stroke is an important part of self-image structuring. A parent can help a child if he strokes in a positive, firm way. A husband or wife can help nurture each other's image if they avoid put-downs and learn the gentle art of verbal stroking. In business, this art can motivate men to achievement. The ability to listen attentively is one of the most effective strokes that one can give; it requires completely focusing attention on the other person so that he knows that he has been truly listened to and his ideas have been absorbed. Attentiveness enables one to relate to another and to give feedback which shows that the other person's point of view is understood. One of my warmest friends has cultivated the art of stroking or, as he terms it, of "giving himself away." He said to me, "I impulsively try to give little bits of myself every day to other people. I look for opportunities to write a note of appreciation, to drop a word of praise in the right place, or to show interest, understanding, and tolerance when I am talking to someone."

In a business context, a man gives *himself* away, not his money or his time. Within your chosen work, giving yourself aways is not really a matter of generosity—it is the basis of successful living. I have often heard men in the life insurance business give testimony to the "law" of life that we enrich ourselves most when we give ourselves most fully and freely. One multimillion-dollar producer said, "I find it impossible to give myself away without getting back more than I gave, provided I give with no thought of reward." While he is well rewarded financially for his efforts, there is no dollar sign in his mind when he serves others.

Even though external stroking can be an important factor in life, internal stroking can be more important. The truth is that recognition by others cannot be depended upon, but we can always recognize ourselves. An entertainer may be applauded hundreds of times each week, but he may find life unsatisfying off stage. The ability to stroke ourselves is related to our self-image. We have to feel good about ourselves, about what we are doing; we have to love ourselves before we can properly stroke ourselves.

Self-stroking means that you put yourself up instead of down; that you take pride and pleasure in yourself and your achievements; that you consciously pat yourself on the back for the good things you are doing; that you do those things which give you joy instead of those things which give you pain; that you have compassion for yourself; and that you recognize yourself for your good works and give thanks for your blessings. The important point about self-stroking is that how we feel about ourselves during the day is a major part of life itself, and through the process of realization we can enjoy the experience of being in charge of how we feel.

Self-esteem is a basic need of man and each of us constantly strives for a sense of worth as a person. Unless a person is in the process of growth—vertically and horizontally—he will lack a sense of purpose and meaningful goals. As he suffers negative responses to his experiences and to stress, his self-esteem lowers; he begins to suffer internally. A basic key to increasing our self-esteem lies in our ability to justifiably receive external stroking in the form of financial and psychological rewards, and to realize internally the knowledge that we are doing something worth doing. A sense of inner worth is crucial to the development of a healthy self-image, and it's our own responsibility to see that we get our share of strokes.

Our Level of Competence

It is quite natural for a man to develop zones within which he operates his personal and working life and in which he feels comfortable. These have been called "comfort zones" because they constitute a range of performance or activity within which a person can function and feel comfortable and operate without tension. For example, a golfer who shoots 80 for 18 holes as his basic game can score three or four shots better or worse than 80 and feel satisfied; he is operating within a comfort area. If his score is either above or below this range, his performance may be affected by tension and can be impaired.

Far too often in business a comfort area of performance is well below a man's potential. It is at this juncture that men may accept mediocrity as a way of life. As their basic financial needs are met, they pull in their horns and accept the status quo—they cease to grow. Often the man who adjusts to this below-par level of performance adjusts to circumstances. He is like hot wax which is poured into a mold and which then hardens. At this point he tends to do what is expected, not more and not less. He does his job, but he lacks the enthusiasm and drive to improve it. Increasingly, his business experiences are repetitive rather than cumulative, and he does not seek change. What he really seeks is security, the safety of his job and the tangible things of life. He loses the knowledge and the thrill of what his own growth can be like, and he adapts himself to someone else's standards and someone else's goals.

A man who has established a below-par comfort zone will usually resist any attempt to make more productive use of his potential, either by himself or someone else. He becomes set in his ways and he resists with great vigor those who would presume to change that fact. Realistically, reexamining a zone of performance which is well below a person's ability can be a very painful experience. We really don't like to stir ourselves up and we use defense mechanisms to protect our ego. The greater the spread between performance and potential, the more we rationalize.

In business, this comfort area constitutes a level of performance which is fenced in by a man's appraisal of his own capacities, by his self-image. If this appraisal is a poor one, the results can sometimes be disastrous, for lack of use of potential can develop into inertia. For example, the older a person gets, the more he withdraws use of his potentials, and the greater the likelihood that energy which could be developed for self-realization will become a destructive and disintegrating force. One of my closest friends said to me recently, "During my life I have been active in business, social, and community pursuits. I was president of my college alumni, on the boards of various organizations, busy with the children and with a wide range of activities. I decided in my fifties that I should taper off a little and not push as hard. I find, however, that our social activities are now quite limited. I'm not in these other activities, and instead of doing more reading, exercise, and constructive things with the extra time, I'm doing less and less of everything."

The process of realizing potential is for those men who

have potential, who want to use it, and who will not accept a second-rate performance for themselves. Such a man is motivated to use what he has. He seeks his own goals and his limits are set by his own potentials. He seeks a level of competence consistent with his abilities, and he is willing to give of himself and to risk himself in order to achieve that goal. An inadequate level of performance can restrict a man's creative ability—his ability to motivate people, to enjoy his work, to keep abreast of his job. The mind which is not fully engaged does not call upon the resources of imagination, enthusiasm, optimism, skill, and increased energy levels which are available to it. There is no need to, for the man has banked the furnace and the call for energy is minimal. The beginning of a new level of competence lies in our own self-awareness and in the development of a wholesome self-image that contains a high degree of self-esteem, truth, positive response, and an internal support system which responds to change. Once a man has tasted the intrinsic rewards of his own growth and has developed a personal philosophy to sustain that growth, he will be reluctant to return to mediocrity if he is capable of something more than that.

Component 3—The Image of Winning and a New Level of Competence

A vital element in vertical and horizontal growth is a man's feeling that he is in fact winning in his life. He pictures himself as successful. The basic support system for a winning feeling lies in the process of realization itself, which develops not only the extrinsic rewards of compensation, recognition, and prestige, but also the intrinsic values of inner worth and a sense of self-esteem. This support system develops a high degree of energy and a well-rounded intellect. Out of commitment to this system come two vital characteristics: first, a feeling of winning; and, second, the capacity of a man to see himself at a new level of competence.

The Feeling of Winning

An objective of the winning feeling is to recapture, to think about, and to mentally embellish the feelings of success. Stated simply, we dwell on success and not on failure. The expectation of winning frees the system from doubts and from negative responses. It enables a man to bring his entire self to bear on a particular problem. He is not split or divided. He is able to put his whole heart, mind, and body into the task at hand. The development of the winning feeling is a major key in growth. Once he has it, a man concentrates his powers and holds nothing back from the particular job at hand. The concentration of power that occurs under these circumstances is truly remarkable, and the results are clearly evidenced by the man who has a winning streak.

We frequently see a winning streak develop in the sports world. A prominent tennis figure, fighter, or golfer will win several consecutive major events. There is no question but that he expects to win, and because of this he magnetizes his condition, he utilizes his creative powers, and releases them to attain his goal. William James, the psychologist, said, "Our belief at the beginning of a doubtful undertaking is the one thing that insures the successful outcome of our venture." The winning streak is the crowning achievement of dedication, talent, and the expectation of success.

Self-esteem is a basic need of man and there is no judgment more important than the one a man passes on himself. The winner feels self-confident and successful; he is in fact successful, and he knows that he is because he stops to savor many small successes in the course of a week. The winner feeds his self-image through the process of realizing his potential; he leaves little to chance in structuring his self-image. Through his philosophy and purpose, his faith and enjoyment of his work, and his capacity to respond positively to pressure, he builds a positive mind. He reinforces and fuels this positive mind through goals which are challenging and which are further developed through visualization. Then, through activity and momentum, he sustains his personal growth and, if he gets his second wind, continues to increase it until it may reach a startling dimension. The cumulative nature of this activity leads to the image of success and to success itself. This image of success is fragile and cannot be long maintained if growth is halted. The winning feeling does not develop accidentally; it is the mark of a professional and is based on thought processes and attitudes which must be constantly reinforced through activity.

I become what I think about. This is another associative phrase to be used in connection with the winning feeling and the self-image. It is interpreted as:

Through the process of my own potential I intend to develop a strong self-image and to call forth constantly the felling of success. Because I become what I think about, I'm going to see myself as a positive, successful, person, earning all of those intrinsic and extrinsic rewards that I desire so deeply.

Seeing a New Level of Competence

The ultimate result of the feeling of winning is often reflected in a desire to reach a new level of competence in one's chosen work. As previously mentioned, the ability of a man to see himself at a new level of competence is one of the most difficult tasks of life. There is a natural human tendency to seek stability and security and to find a stable level of performance in an activity. Once this pattern is set, it becomes difficult to change.

There is, however, an enormous interest, particularly in men between the ages of twenty-five and forty-five, to grow vertically in their work. Much of this drive is motivated by the desire to earn a greater income and the ability to enjoy what money will buy for a man and his family. The urge toward a new level of competence is supported again by visualization. A young man, age 28, with the need and the desire to progress vertically in his work, said to me after several sessions, "Does visualization really work? I don't really understand it." My reply was:

"Visualization as a tool in the process of potential is extremely difficult to describe. In a sense, it is like trying to tell a person what an avocado tastes like when that person has never tasted an avocado. In the same way, visualization must be used and practiced before a man can truly understand what it means and how it applies to this particular situation. It's a lot more than pictures. For example, if I dream of 'Jeannie with the light brown hair,' when I awaken from that dream, Jeannie will not be there, of course, but if I dream of a Jeannie neatly filling out a bikini, it is quite probable that the next day I'll be on the lookout for her and try to arrange a date with her.

"Visualization also implies more than just the ability to vividly imagine a particular scene or set of circumstances; it involves the way we feel about ourselves and our purpose and meaning in life. In a broad sense, therefore, visualization lies in the power of your mind to collect information, to sort it out, to apply your past experiences, and to create new solutions. It operates very much like a magnifying glass which, when properly focused, concentrates light from the sun and raises enough heat to burn a hole in the object on which the rays are focused. The glass, however, must be held steady before the power is fully developed. When visualization is used correctly, you begin to feel or see yourself performing an action, and you go ahead and do it; this picture or feeling helps bring it into actual existence. In essence, this is a total thought process which begins to concentrate on the direction you are taking and gives meaning to your goals; it accelerates your development. In its broad sense, visualization is an art form, and some people are better at it than others. In terms of your growth, it can be developed in such a way that it can assist materially in the development of your vertical progress in your work.

"I am sure that you will not find it hard to create a picture of yourself as being in control of your life rather than having external events control it. You can imagine and feel deeply that you are at the helm of your own ship and determining your own course. In this picture you act, rather than react to life, because you are always in control. Exactly how you create this image is for you to decide. Perhaps you might use a mental screen, similar to one you use at home on which to project your slides. You might then picture on that screen how you would look and act when you control your own destiny. This goal, this picture, should be embellished, defined, and desired to the point where you can feel it happening. The point is that given an adequate support system, this goal will become a reality, provided its visualization is continued for a long enough period of time to become a habit, to become part of you."

When a man begins to see himself at a new level, he consciously sets new goals and collects and sorts out facts and problems as he views them. But when he stops consciously thinking about the matter, his mind continues to consider the problem. A major part of this new image develops and matures beyond his power of conscious control. He has a "think tank" which works for him and in his behalf, provided it is fed the right material.

The Group Self-Image

One of the most exciting things that can occur in a group of people with a common project is the development of *esprit de corps*. The term connotes dedication and belief in a common purpose—a missionary zeal and an excitement which is felt and communicated by members of a group. It is not a common occurrence. It is most conducive to effective, winning performance. An example of *esprit de corps* occurred when Vince Lombardi was the head coach of the Green Bay Packers. Through his leadership and his dedication, he molded his team together into a unit which was virtually unbeatable. The mark of a great leader lies in his ability to get his men to see themselves at a new level of competence. A friend said to me recently, "Certain coaches can get men to play over their heads." Where *esprit de corps* exists, it will be recognized in the way it touches men's minds and the power it generates. It is, in a sense, a group self-image.

Esprit de corps develops within a framework of expectation.

The performance of a man is very much affected by what is expected (or demanded) of him, and a leader of men supplies such a framework of expectation. The leader who develops this atmosphere is himself in the process of growth. His message springs from inner strength, his "center." He is totally authentic and believable. His message cannot be faked; it comes from the core of his integrity. A very astute executive put it well when he said, "When a man becomes a manager, he should forget he is a manager. His overriding interest must be the growth of the men under his guidance."

The primary function is to lead and develop men. Instead of people being problems and costs, they become a company's most valuable resource. The leader recognizes that men need to be motivated, that they can be turned off or turned on by a job or a boss. Under the direction of a leader, men can acquire the habit of achievement. Under a "manager," they can also acquire the habit of defeat. A leader of men is himself an achiever. His central strength in motivating others rests on his belief in the dignity and potential of the man he is working with and the fact that he himself is in the process of realizing his own potential. He is a giver in the true sense of the word.

The leader wants not conformance but performance, which is based on raising a man's sights in a way that motivates him to a higher level of competence. He supplies the guidelines, the incentives, the inspiration that makes a man want to raise his vertical achievement index. In essence, the leader supplies an atmosphere for self-respect and productivity, which can occur only through the self-motivation and self-direction of the man.

Summary

One of the outstanding achievements in any businessman's life is the development of a wholesome self-esteem, a sense of inner worth. It is not a gift; it is not inherited. Men earn it when they seek their own potential. It is a battle to be constantly rewon, and its victories are the development of a positive response and the qualities of enthusiasm, courage, love, optimism, empathy, and tolerance, to name but a few.

A satisfying and adequate self-image nurtures inner worth. It also defines the boundaries of a man's performance. When the self-concept is fluid and growing, it is a constructive force; when it hardens at a level well below potential, it can be destructive or at least unsatisfying.

The process of realizing potential is presented as a support system for an adequate self-image. It is designed to pro-

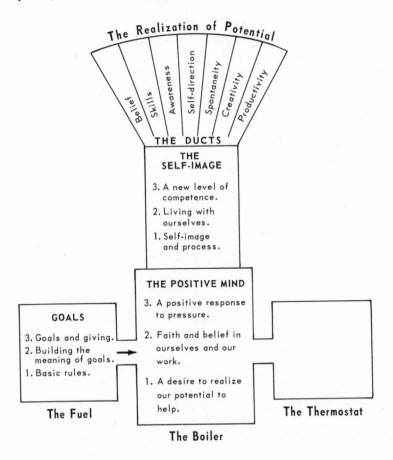

duce both external rewards in the form of money and recognition and the intrinsic feelings of self-worth. It builds a self-concept with an enduring foundation.

An enlarging self-concept tends to produce a winning feeling and a growing degree of competence in one's work. Through visualization and the development of strong goals, coupled with a strong desire to grow, a new level of competence becomes possible. A positive image opens up the channels of the mind to assist in reaching this new level of achievement.

Through the key conditioner *I become what I think,* we can be reminded to build a mental picture of being successful and positive in everything that we do, and to take credit for our successes. In effect, the goal is to be a winner.

The next step in this process is the determination of the level of activity and the degree of energy to be produced. In short, how badly do we want to win, and what controls might be used?

5

Checkpoint 4 — the mind

Two men, with approximately equal talents, may develop the components of potential on approximately the same basis, yet one man may produce two or three times the result of the other. This can be closely observed in sales work, where a man's work and his results are measurable; either he makes sales or he doesn't, and results can be closely compared.

A senior executive for a large chemicals corporation said recently, "The men we hire in our work are all technically competent. What we're looking for are men who have the desire, who are interested in their work, and who want to do a job." He added, "Look, we can't make these men want to grow; this has to come from them; they have to have the desire themselves."

The differences in motivation between one man and another—the reasons why one man achieves great heights while another does not—are indeed complex. In the Bible's Book of Psalms, David says, ". . . I am fearfully and wonderfully made . . ." and this is the substance of one of the most important aspects of our own special uniqueness, our individual capabilities. If we are stuck in a groove while another man succeeds, should we throw up our hands and say in despair that this man has a God-given gift, or that this individual was lucky and that his parents had him live in an air of great expectation in his childhood, or that he was in competitive activities in school which developed his drive, or he had inherited his drive from his parents? Do we excuse ourselves and say that the drive factor is an individual matter, and a man either has it or he doesn't have it, and there really isn't too much we can do about it?

This chapter is entitled "The Mind" because so much of the difference in performance between men of approximately equal ability results from certain mental attitudes toward their work and their own potential. These components are controllable and determine the amount of the "fuel" used to create energy and productivity.

For example, assume three carpenters are hard at work on a building and are asked what they are doing. One man replies, "I'm putting the framework up for this building." The second man says, "I'm building a room which will be 20 by 30 feet." The third man says, "I'm working on a school for children where they will come to learn and play." The third man has a concept and a vision of what he is doing, which is more meaningful than that of his associates. From a career viewpoint, this meaningful, broad-range involvement with one's work and life represents an energizer which develops the intensity of potential.

Three components will be considered which develop the level and intensity of a man's performance: commitment and dedication, the use of time, and rising above one's own limitations.

Component 1—Commitment and Dedication

How can a man begin to develop his own special level of energy, intellect, and potential in his chosen career? The words "I am committed" are an important key to the degree of development of potential. When a man is committed to a course of action, his course is charted. For example, an outside salesman who is committed to seeing a certain number of people each week has to worry no longer about fifteen extraneous facets of his business, which may sap his energy. His overriding commitment is to see the required number of people per week and all other considerations become secondary at that point. He thus becomes concentrated in his efforts. He has no need to consciously separate the wheat from the chaff. His course and his direction are clear. He is committed.

As a result of this commitment, this man brings all of himself into play. He automatically coordinates and integrates all of his past experience, his education, his training, his skills. He focuses the spotlight of his entire being on a single objective. In so doing, he calls forth latent potentials and creativity. He makes it possible for a new level of competence to begin to develop.

In the same way, the ability of a businessman to commit himself fully to his job has a marked bearing on the level of his performance. A man who is committed sees his work as an enormously important part of his life. He is aware that he cannot gain greater satisfaction from the job than he is willing to give to it. If he finds that he is not receiving the satisfaction he feels he needs from his job, or is not in fact realizing his potential in that job in spite of the fact that he is giving everything to it, he may well begin to consider other alternatives. It is not possible, however, for him to arrive at this conclusion unless he has been fully committed to his job in the first place. If his efforts have been half-hearted, if he has not totally involved himself in his work, he cannot hope for true satisfaction under any circumstances. He is therefore not qualified to evaluate his potential in that work, or to judge whether he should or should not change that job.

Full commitment by a businessman brings out qualities which would otherwise remain submerged. The sum total of his past experience, as well as his presently developed abilities, integrates a man so that he can function at a high level. The greater the degree of the commitment, the more these powers are brought into play, and the more effective they are in utilizing potential.

Every businessman is aware of commitment when he has occasion to hire a new employee. For example, in one case, a new man does his job half-heartedly; he is there to do a day's work for a day's pay, and little more. He is basically uninvolved and uncommitted to his job. It is merely a way of making a living. Another employee with the same job, however, sees it as a challenge. He is fully involved with it and tries to find ways to make it more interesting and to do it better and more efficiently. Through his commitment, this individual begins to grow, he begins to enlarge his self-concept, his self-esteem, and he opens up the creative powers of his mind. His actions become apparent to his superiors, and when the right job opens up he is asked to accept it. One man, in this case, looks at a half a glass of water as half-empty, while the other man looks at it as half-full.

Commitment and dedication are therefore closely related to potential. If a man commits himself to his job, he pledges himself to it. He then begins to concentrate his activities. Because of his commitment, he may then become dedicated to his work. The intensity of this dedication—of being absorbed and devoted—to his vertical potential is a decision that each man must make for himself, and the degree of commitment and dedication will vary widely among businessmen. For example, a very successful contractor, age 45, who scores himself at a level of 9 vertically, has built up a small business to a net worth of $750,000. He said, "My only problem is that I need greater ability. I put in a twelve-hour day and I thoroughly enjoy my work. I'm not fighting it. I find people and business situations interesting and I enjoy creating capital. As far as potential in other areas of my life is concerned, there is room for improvement, because most of my effort is in my work." I have observed this man on many occasions, and I have never known him to operate in a stressful way, or to be fatigued. While this man works sixty-five hours every week and loves it, he is not the average businessman. Most men to whom I have talked seek a greater level of horizontal growth, but in both cases the principle of commitment and dedication are the same.

The Mastery of One's Work

Dedication—viewed as the ability to be absorbed and devoted to one's work—is a growing requirement for the development of vertical competence. The demands of the business world are increasing so rapidly that the realization of potential more and more requires what might be termed "one-pointedness." Unless a man is dedicated to his work, he can never become a master at it. In fact, in every field of endeavor, the price of success requires the complete and undivided attention of the participant and an absolute dedication to the principles of his career. A man must be free of distractions, contented, and satisfied with his lot, and he must be at peace with himself in order to maintain a high sense of purpose.

The various components in realizing potential lead to the mastery of one's work. They provide a frame of reference for growth. In a sense, these techniques are the scales a master pianist practices each day. According to Ernest Newman, the English music critic, "Beethoven, Wagner, Bach, and Mozart settled down day after day to the job at hand with as much regularity as an accountant settles down each day to his figures. They didn't waste time waiting for inspiration." Their talent lay in their dedication to their work, which made possible the expression of their genius.

The businessman who is dedicated focuses his attention on his chosen work and becomes absorbed by that work. Those men who fulfill themselves vertically in their work are always dedicated. While a man can still develop horizontal competence to a marked degree, a watered-down effort in business will not succeed.

Dedication calls into play the full powers of the mind. Intense concentration causes things to fall into place, and a man will utilize powers of creativity and reasoning which he perhaps did not know that he had. The dedicated professional, in losing himself in his work, can increasingly come to look upon it as a play or a leisure activity. He gains the capacity to do his job simply because he enjoys it. He can express himself through it because he is fully aware of the intrinsic and extrinsic rewards which result from his efforts.

The businessman who seeks fulfillment has an awareness that his personal growth in his chosen work is vital to his well-being and that through his dedication he earns an increasing amount of money with which to benefit his family, while at the same time he develops his own sense of inner worth. Through one-pointedness in his business approach, his potentials increase to where they spill over into other parts of his life. Finally, he increasingly looks at his chosen work more as a leisure activity to which his reactions are responses of a positive nature.

It has been fascinating to talk to men who are masters at their work. They usually are committed to the point where they spend from one to five extra hours per day on the job and love every minute. It appears that extra hours, properly spent, can add value to a man's time, which can be geometric in its effect. In other words, a 20 percent increase in time can expand a businessman's productive output by 100 percent or more. This principle is used extensively by men whose primary goal in life is the development of their vertical potential. It is an important key, which can be used to regulate productive energy, if a man so desires.

Commitment and Dedication to Realizing Potential

The willingness of a man to commit himself to his job affects every component in the development of his potential. In large measure, a commitment is a state of mind, how we look at things. The more clearly a man sees his involvement in his work as critical to his personal development, the more readily he will become fully involved. He becomes more amenable to accepting the negatives of his work—a tough boss, long hours, or continual crises—when he can fully evaluate his basic need for involvement and productivity, as well as his need for self-esteem and a feeling of competence.

In the ultimate sense, a dedicated man gives freely of

himself. By giving the best of himself to his work, he discovers the potentials of his work and himself. However, the degree of his growth will depend on how much of himself he brings to this commitment. If he plunges fully into the job with a positive mind, he utilizes hidden talents and releases abilities and capacities which have been unrealized. Through total career engagement, on a positive basis, a man expands and grows.

A young management man, about 35, recently expressed dissatisfaction with his work and the many problems he has. He currently rates himself at about 4 on the potential scale. He said, "All my life I've heard about how I should use more of my potential. My parents told me this about my school work and so did my teachers. In athletics or golf, or whatever, I was always told I could do better if I worked at it. But I've never been able to come to grips with this problem of my potential. It's depressing." It was obvious that this man was not fully committed to his work and that he was not giving fully of himself. As a result, his thoughts about his job were negative. As we talked briefly about a positive view of his work and the rewards of dedication, he finally said, "I see what you mean. I've been missing the boat." Even a slight shift in mental outlook can sometimes materially alter a career.

When we bring all of ourselves into play—through commitment—the task of goal setting is simplified. When we care enough to do our best, we begin to look for ways to grow and to extend ourselves. Through this growth, our goals enlarge and become more meaningful. In turn, as goals develop and mature, dedication is kept at a high level. There is a compelling interaction between goals and commitment. It's like the song that says, "You can't have one without the other."

As I have said before, commitment materially affects the self-image. A lukewarm career commitment will not work. It will ordinarily be damaging in extrinsic terms (that is, money), and also in a lack of self-esteem and competency. It can therefore affect seriously every facet of a man's business and personal life.

In business, the spark that makes a man brilliant is not

entirely his technical ability or better self-organization. It is not entirely better planning or knowledge. What sets the fire under these qualities is the commitment to serve. This commitment makes a man stand out; it cannot be faked. In the business world, commitment, dedication, and service are what faith, hope, and charity are in the conduct of our lives, and the greatest of these is service.

Component 2—The Use of Time

The utilization of time during the course of a day constitutes one of the prime differences in performance between men of equal abilities. The time of the businessman is measured in terms of dollars. On an hourly basis this breaks down to, say, $10, $15, $20, or more dollars per hour. If, for example, a man is being paid $15 per hour for his time, it can be assumed that he is exercising considerable responsibility and creativity in his work. His employer has no desire to pay $15 per hour if 40 percent of the man's time is spent in performing functions worth $5 per hour. Yet, this is what may happen when $5 functions blend with $15 tasks.

An amusing and pointed example of the value of time was recently told me by a top-flight businessman. He said, "I had only been in business with my father a few years. I was running a very small company that he owned when one day he called me into his office. He told me he was reducing my salary, that hereafter I would receive the same wage the shippers in the plant were receiving. I said, 'I can't live on that wage. I have a wife and children, and besides, I'm not a shipper.' Dad said, 'Where have you been all afternoon?' I replied, 'In the shipping department.' Dad then said, 'Most of the week I've seen you in the shipping department. If you want to be a shipper, that's OK, but that's what your wages will be.' " This man has never forgotten this lesson, and of course he stopped going into the shipping department unless it was necessary.

Disorganization

The inability to structure a working hour of time on the basis of its true value leads to a disorganized schedule, with a substantial impact on potential. In the first place, disorganization leads to the feeling that you have insufficient time to do what you want to do. This leads to the feeling of being rushed and at times to a feeling of panic. No one can work efficiently under these circumstances.

Disorganization also leads to a negative response to pressure—to fear and anxiety. A disorganized man will tend to level out prematurely and thereby affect every component in the process of realizing potential; rather than being in control of himself, events begin to control his day. He ceases to be in charge. A disorganized schedule leads to the postponement of decisions and to nonproductivity. As delay and postponement of important decisions becomes habitual, paralysis sets in. As important tasks continue to be left for mañana, $5.00 tasks add to the mental burdens of the day. Eventually, a man is carrying around in his head the burdens of yesterday, today, and tomorrow, and no one can be productive under these circumstances.

Finally, a disorganized schedule makes it most difficult for a man to progress in his job. Through its adverse effects it inhibits the natural processes of his positive mind and his goal structuring, and impairs his self-image. It causes a stereotyped, repetitive thought process instead of the creative thought process which produces results. These thoughts become an escape mechanism. The salesman sits in his office instead of doing the more difficult job of going out and making calls. The management man sits in his office and plays with figures rather than being on the job motivating men who are under him. Lower-priced work increasingly expands to fill the vacuum created by the nonuse of potential.

A constructive and rewarding exercise for a businessman is to periodically price-evaluate the various functions he has been performing. In this exercise he lists on paper what he has done on the basis of its cost per hour. One side of the paper represents $5.00-an-hour time, while the other side represents his own hourly rate. He then lists the various functions he has been performing each day under each of these categories. The results are often surprising and can result in a reassignment of priorities. The man who desires to grow and increase his competence vertically must be somewhat ruthless in evaluating his own time. The human inclination to do the easier job must be vigorously resisted because it is inimical to the realization of potential. The simple method of pricing what a man is doing with his time simplifies what could otherwise be a difficult task. It will usually result in the reassignment of his priorities.

Unless a man is consciously growing, he will unconsciously turn toward less expensive tasks, to those tasks which he is not supposed to be doing. These tasks, of course, are easier and more enjoyable, and he has little trouble performing them.

Priorities

A basic requirement in structuring business time is the allocation of priorities. Creative energy—which is the essence of the more highly paid jobs—flourishes when there is time for mature, deliberate consideration of important matters. In other words, if a man is bogged down with tasks which represent $5.00-an-hour time, he becomes a victim of confused, hurried thinking.

The old adage "haste makes waste" might also be used in the context of "haste makes poor business decisions." Actually, a continuous, frenzied pace almost guarantees disaster in any field of activity. The creation of priorities—in terms of vertical potential—will relate to the overall importance of the task and its dollar value to the business. In other words, those jobs whose values are not equal to, or are above, a man's hourly rate of pay must be eliminated or delegated to someone else. If they are not, a man's rating suffers. The president of an automobile agency told me recently, "I rate myself about a 5. I really haven't learned to be a manager yet; I'm still a doer. I don't delegate a sufficient number of my tasks." I have observed this fine man move in his work at an unusually rapid pace. He admits he is somewhat frustrated and that his success has come in spite of his inability to delegate. An employee should not lose favor with his boss if he insists that he should not do work which others can do at a lower pay scale.

The creation of an organized daily schedule which allows time for creative thought should be practical if that schedule is based on a man's hourly rate of pay. This can automatically eliminate many functions which have previously crowded his calendar, allowing him more time for the important tasks during a day.

The ability to establish priorities develops potential. Under these circumstances a man tends to become better than he was the day before. In a sense, if his time is worth $15 per hour, he is trying to give his employer $20 worth of value if he can do it without stress. Such an approach is looked for by employers, and unquestionably leads to career growth.

A forcing system is basic to the efficient use of time and the setting of priorities. In a sense, it might be likened to the 20/80 law, which states that a few critical efforts (around 20 percent) generally produce the great bulk of results (around 80 percent). For example, in the life insurance business, the critical key to success is the ability of a salesman to prospect, to build a supply of people with buying power whom he can reach most efficiently. Most men who leave the business do so because they are unable to solve this major problem. As a result, they vacillate and waste so much time trying to get in front of people that they are forced out of business. As a practical matter, the difficulty arises because 80 to 90 percent of most producers' time is spent in selling life insurance and 10 to 20 percent on prospecting. A proper forcing system leads a man to concentrate his efforts on the critical problem of prospecting, so that he begins to reverse these percentages. His major effort then revolves around the prospecting problem. Forcing goals, which are critical to a job, have a great effect on priorities and the use of a man's time. They also have immense influence on the development of potential.

Most men who must manage themselves have great difficulty in setting forcing goals which fully develop their potential. It appears that the more a man is left to his own devices, the greater his resistance to the adoption of a forcing system. As a friend once said, "Too many men want to eat the meal but don't want to wash the dishes." Perhaps this occurs because it is far easier to move downhill than to climb uphill. In terms of the process of realizing potential, a man's willingness to do what has to be done is enhanced when he understands that the price tag for letting his own personal achievement index fall is too great. Stated positively, a good rating is self-fulfilling.

Time and Leisure Activity

Assuming that an hour of time is efficiently used, it has been suggested that one of the options open for individual growth is simply to add more hours to the working day. There are those men who are so dedicated to work, whose work is so enjoyable to them, that they work twelve to fifteen hours a day with great pleasure. This is often true of scientists, musicians, artists who have reached a high level of performance. Their vocation, in a sense, has become their recreation. There are also those men in the business world who have an enormous dedication to their work, not because of a compulsion for power or money, but because they thoroughly enjoy what they are doing.

Another fine businessman, age 65, owns three different companies and is busier than he has ever been in his life. I asked him recently, "You're over age 65 now, you have more money than you'll ever need, why don't you retire?" His answer was, "I believe the only true pleasure in this world is the joy of accomplishment, for me or for anyone. A vacation is fun, like drinking a cold drink is fun, but you can't drink cold drinks constantly. On the other hand, nothing is more refreshing than to take a good vacation when you've worked your butt off." To this man, his work is a leisure activity, and there's nothing in the world he would rather do.

In general, a score of 7 or above on the potential scale has seemed to indicate job satisfaction and a reasonable use of time. But the use of time in one's work to further increase vertical potential above that point is very much a private affair.

In terms of the process of realizing potential, the enjoyment of one's work to the point where it becomes a leisure activity magnetizes a man's situation and brings out the best in him. It has a material effect on growth and productive output. Whether a man chooses to achieve the hoped for geometric effect that extra hours may give is entirely an individual decision.

Time and Goals

It is difficult to imagine the efficient use of time if goals are not properly structured. For example, if goals are not sharply defined, it becomes difficult to concentrate and far too easy to go off on tangents. An executive said recently, "I have this plant superintendent who spends all his day putting out fires. He is driving us crazy because he can't seem to get organized. He works hard, but he wastes so much motion."

Many successful men use a very simple but specific technique in connection with their goal setting, which enables them to stay on the track and which eliminates haste and disorganization from their thinking. Their technique is very simple: They make specific plans for each week before that week starts. The various tasks to be done on a given day are then committed to paper in order of priority, which is strictly adhered to. This preparation is done before the day starts. During the day, each task is completed in its order of priority; as it is finished, it is crossed off the list and the next job is then undertaken. By the end of the day, those jobs which are not completed are carried forward on the schedule of tasks to be achieved the following day, again according to their priority. Many men have said that this simple, specific plan develops the power of intense concentration and frees the mind for creative activity.

Perhaps you've heard the story of Charlie Schwab, the former president of Bethlehem Steel, one of the few men ever to be paid $1 million a year. Schwab was fretting because he couldn't seem to get enough done. Details and minor matters kept crowding in on his time, keeping him from getting to more important tasks. He asked a management consultant what to do about it. The consultant handed Schwab a blank sheet of paper. "Write down," he said, "the six most important things you intend to do tomorrow. Tomorrow morning start on item one and work on it until it's finished. Then go on to the next item." The steel executive tried the idea. He found it so helpful he recommended it to his associates and, reportedly, sent the consultant a check for $25,000 in appreciation.

Obviously, the use of time by a businessman will vary widely, depending upon the particular nature of his job. Some of the jobs scheduled each day are repetitive and are, in a sense, clerical in nature. However, as the businessman moves into the area of creativity and decision making, which is inherent in the higher paid job, he must begin to organize himself to determine his daily goals, and the means he will use to meet those goals. He has to begin to take charge of himself. He becomes increasingly responsible for the effective use of his time. There are some specifics which can be helpful in maximizing the use of time:

1. Allow ample time for the important events on your schedule each day. No task should be handled in an atmosphere of haste. It is important that the mind not be cluttered and led into a state of panic by trying to catch up. The businessman whose tasks are not clearly laid out, who becomes hurried and disorganized, spoils his creative thinking. He engages in repetitive, stereotyped thought processes. He impairs his creativity. On the other hand, the man who has completed his scheduled work is able to exercise creativity. He is in a position to experiment, to weigh alternatives, to consider fully the solutions to difficult problems. Disorganization during the day almost always insures failure.

2. Eliminate those items from your calendar which are not economically worth your time, or assign them to a subordinate. Again, if a man is doing a job worth $4.00 an hour when he is being paid $10, $15, or $20 an hour, he is obviously squandering his time. There is, as mentioned, great value in price-evaluating business functions.

3. Do not permit yourself to be interrupted frequently during an assigned task. Starting and stopping a particular job in order to answer questions, or to answer the telephone, or to embark on some other project can materially diminish effectiveness and concentration. This leads to disorganization, a feeling on the part of a man that events are controlling him and that therefore his time is wasted.

4. Keep your desk clean. Every paper that clutters up a desk, every letter that remains unanswered, every memo that remains unfiled continually reminds the businessman that he is behind in his work, and this inevitably contributes to a feeling of disorganization. One of the fundamental objectives of the process of developing potential is a clear mind, which permits creativity and growth to expand.

5. Focus your efforts on one job at a time and in the order of its priority. Concentration maximizes the value of time. Jumping from job to job destroys momentum and requires excessive use of energy to get the mental machinery in motion each time a new task is started.

6. Simplify the complicated jobs and goals. Breaking a big job down into its components makes its accomplishment possible and effectively uses time. For example, a yearly sales objective may seem unsurmountable, but on a daily basis it may mean only that a man must call on three good prospects per day. This daily objective may be quite attainable and reasonable.

7. Learn to pace yourself. Each man has rhythm peculiar to himself. Rhythm, or the "beat," is the most basic element in music. Without it, music is a disorganized mass of discordant notes. The baton of the conductor or the sticks of the drummer maintain the orchestra's rhythm. This also applies to most physical and mental activities in daily life. The businessman's

"baton" lies in his own recognition of the dollar value of his time, developed as he engages in realizing his own potential.

Key Conditioner

An associative phrase, *Time is money,* is used to recall the need to price-evaluate time and to set a schedule of priorities each day, with full attention being given to one task at a time.

Component 3—Rising above One's Own Limitations

As pointed out before, one of the key objectives in realizing potential is a positive response to pressure and the development of emotions of hope, faith, belief, enthusiasm, empathy, tolerance, etc. In the course of his daily activity, the businessman creates mental images and records his thoughts on figurative tapes, which play over and over again. These imaginary tapes register his interpretation of events, which he may come to regard as absolute authority and which may be negative recordings. These may be associated with the use of his own potential, the amount of money that he is making, or the way he feels about his company or his boss. The more he fights and struggles, the harder it becomes to modify these interpretations. In essence, what happens is that the subconscious part of the mind seeks to solve the problems, but because it has been programmed by mental images, its reaction is machinelike—and therefore limited in scope—and can run out of control.

It has also been pointed out that, since the subconscious mind is very much like a computer which stores and processes data, it is quite possible for this machine to take over and control our lives. In the absence of definitive and conscious goal setting on the part of the businessman, the mechanical mind controls, creativity is inhibited, and a businessman's actions tend to become stereotyped and repetitive in nature. The objective is to relegate the mechanical mind to its appropriate

place, which is to take orders and not to give them. Nevertheless, the mechanical mind is essential, and is a most valuable
tool in realization of potential. It is indispensable in coping
with the problems of life. In a sense, however, it's like a television set which can run continuously and which can preoccupy
and distract the businessman. Left to itself, it creates and tries
to solve problems, but cannot do it without having the proper
input.

It helps a businessman if he occasionally stops to analyze
his mechanical reactions as he goes through his working day.
Just as he determines whether tension, physical tension, is
robbing him of his energy, it is just as possible for his thoughts
to affect his efficiency and his productive work. Notice during
the day whether your mind is concentrated on the task at hand
or is continually wandering and being distracted by thoughts
which have no particular bearing on your work. It is a fact that
people who cannot concentrate generally prove to be
inefficient. Become aware of the tapes in your mind which are
playing over and over again, and which are not worth the
expenditure of energy. Very often these tapes feed back negative thinking and fears. During the course of this exercise,
when it becomes apparent that useless thoughts are interfering
with your concentration, order them to stop. You will become
aware that they need not play over and over continuously and
that you can control them.

Exercise—Eliminating Extraneous Thoughts

A good practice exercise in this regard is to attempt to be
aware of the essence of each activity that you engage in
throughout the day. Take a new look at those jobs which you
have regarded as mechanical, or boring, or unpleasant.
Periodically throw yourself into these jobs and feel them and
experience them. Most jobs have a great deal of routine con-
nected with them. It is also very easy to look at many aspects of
a job as unpleasant. When you feel this happening, give your-

self wholeheartedly to doing these tasks and you will find that, in most cases, they can be quite enjoyable. The feeling that certain parts of our work are distasteful is a negative attitude which disappears when we stop resisting and come to grips with them. Once you discover the interesting aspects of these jobs, you will not be distracted by errant thoughts.

Action and Reaction

It is a basic law of life that for every action, no matter how slight, there is in some way or other a reaction. In many ways this law is predictable. For example, when a ball squarely meets a bat, its direction will be reversed. On the other hand, the effects of many actions are delayed, as with smoking cigarettes, where the effects on health will not be observable for 20, 30, or 40 years. The fact remains, however, that for each cigarette smoked, there is a tiny negative effect on the human physical system.

A basic objective in realizing potential lies in a man's capacity to act, rather than to react, to the events and circumstances which are occurring around him each day. His aim is to become an actor rather than a reactor. If a man reacts most of the time, he inhibits his creative thought processes. When a man allows his thinking to be taken over by reactions to an irritable boss, economic circumstances, or other pressures, he becomes a captive of events rather than a creator of them. He increasingly loses the ability to concentrate on his problems in a positive way. His mind becomes occupied with events of the past and the projection of future events. It is quite possible for this cycle to continue to the point where he spends most of his time in anticipation and worry about events that might happen, instead of living and experiencing life in the present.

The capacity of the mind to act rather than to react, and thereby to improve efficiency, is an attitude which can be consciously cultivated. The essence of this attitude or feeling lies in objectivity and not in subjectivity. A surgeon cannot perform his work efficiently if he is personally involved with the patient, even though he may be dealing with the life of the person on the operating table. He must be totally dispassionate and objective. Only then can he do his job properly. In the same way, the businessman, although being in the fire of business life, cannot permit himself to be burned continuously by the events around him. Therefore he ceases to be actively involved and withdraws from the matter. It is actually true that, with most of our problems, the moment we say, "I'm tired of worrying, let the worst happen," the negative response will lose much of its power. It is perfectly practical for a businessman to cease to be involved personally in many of the activities which are draining his energy. If he wishes to rise above his own limitations, he can. In this way, he acquires objectivity, which enables him to handle problems efficiently.

The ability of a businessman to regain objectivity, to stay in control of a situation and to avoid being tossed about by circumstances, is an important factor in realizing potential. An excellent technique is that of consciously directing the mind to rise above the problems which are causing worry and confusion. The next time you have a serious business problem, order yourself to rise above subjective thoughts, to transcend them. As you develop this capacity, you assume control of your mind; you become an actor rather than a reactor.

The Development of Habits

The tendency to reject new ideas and experiences as one grows older has been commented upon. Not only does the resistance to new ideas increase, but there is a tendency to move in an ever-narrowing circle of friends with common political and economic viewpoints. The acquisition of new attitudes and skills seems pointless. We are, of course, creatures of habit, established through repetition, and men are creators of habit just as machines are creators of momentum. Habit tends to form its own momentum. It is impossible to imagine life without momentum, for airplanes would be grounded and no vehicle could move. Without the momentum of habit, every decision we make would be a new one, and so we, too, would grind to a halt. It is a fact that we are what we are because we have formed the habit of being that way, and the only way to change is through the establishment of new habits.

It is readily observable that man may become increasingly controlled by constrictive habits which limit his potential and which deprive him of new experiences and flexibility. On the other hand, the components of potential realization involve consideration of habits which augment rather than diminish the use of potential. For example, when a man commits himself to realizing his own potential, he begins to assume control of himself and of his own direction. The goal to think positively or to structure goals carefully is powerfully linked to a total process, and as a man consciously continues to work on that goal each day, he will reach the stage where finally something wonderful happens—a desired goal has become a habit and the decision does not have to be made that day because it is automatic.

Certainly, one of the basic means of altering undesirable habits lies in the area of goal structuring. For example, the clear definition of a goal is essential. As previously discussed, one must forget generalities like "I want to be a better manager" or "I want to be a better salesman." Instead, the goal might be, "I want to develop four capable department heads this year." Given this known specific, the mind can then begin to implement the tasks necessary to accomplish it and can effect the changes in habits necessary to do so. Proper career habits are easier to make if the end result is clearly known and much desired.

The second element of establishing a new habit is through repetition. The more frequently an act is performed, the more it becomes a part of an individual's personality. Repetition is one of the elements suggested in a program described in the next section of this chapter. The establishment of the new habit requires that the act be repeated over a sufficient period of time so that it will become automatic.

Programming the Potential Habit

Throughout this book, certain associative and very simple phrases and sentences have been used to recall the basic components developed in this book. These associative phrases can sometimes be useful in enabling a man to reach a new level of competence.

When a businessman attempts to relearn or practice one or more of the components in his growth, it is clear that new mental recordings must be made which will supersede those fixed ideas not in accord with his purpose. This is a conscious decision, and recognizes that the mind is not only receptive to what we feed it, but that it will also immediately begin to translate our thoughts into their physical equivalents.

The establishment of new recordings which maximize a man's potential is a key to reaching a new level of competence. Yet, it can be the greatest problem in a business career because of the tendency to constrict performance into a groove well below potential. Actions and substitutes which are inimical to the development of a man's potential can quickly become habits—and most difficult to change. Realizing potential requires self-understanding, commitment to both the extrinsic and intrinsic rewards that come through growth, the free and full use of the mechanical and imaginative aspects of the mind, and sufficient repetition so that the message of potential is fully absorbed by the mind. The programming method recommended in this section is simple, straightforward, and beneficial. This particular program attempts to emphasize the highlights of this book and provide positive input. It may be changed to meet an individual's own specific aims.

Assume that your subject is a businessman who, for one reason or another, does not score himself a passing mark on the scale of his own potential and that he wishes to alter this fact. If he uses the suggested program it should be read carefully each night just before turning out the light, and should be read over a period of approximately five to six weeks. At the end of this period, the saturation of the mind should be sufficient to begin the structuring of new and beneficial attitudes. The basis of this program is repetition, intensified by motivation and emotion. It is suggested that the material be read slowly, with frequent pauses to let ideas or images sink in. The objective is to recall the meaning of these associative phrases through visualization and emphasis.

Exercise — Developing New Habits

> *Read this each night just before turning out the lights.*
> *Read it with the greatest meaning possible.*

Relax before you read this. Breathe deeply and rhythmically. Visualize a pleasant scene. Relax your eyelids. Then read slowly, pausing for a moment after each paragraph:

I strongly desire to dedicate myself to the process of realizing my own unique potentials and to be in control of my life and moving toward my ideal of what I can be.

To reinforce my desire to grow, I will recall that *Every day, in every way, I'm getting better and better.* By this, I mean that each and every day I'm improving in the way I look, feel, and act, and I can actually feel this growth.

Faith and belief in myself and my chosen work are vital to my self-confidence and success. To keep this constantly in front of me I will use the thought *positive thoughts benefit me.*

Positive thoughts of optimism, enthusiasm, courage, hope, and belief in myself benefit me. These positive thoughts benefit my health; they bring happiness and peace of mind and are vital to achieving my goals.

I want to dedicate myself to my work, and to regard it as my cause. I strongly desire to grow vertically in my work through a philosophy of giving and of service to others.

I visualize myself pursuing my work with energy, enthusiasm, and genuine pleasure, and with a quiet confidence that radiates to other people.

A vital part of my positive mind lies in a positive response to pressure, by which I mean I meet pressure with emotions of courage, faith, belief, hope, and optimism. By engaging in the process of realizing my potential, I will encourage and develop the emotions of courage and love.

So as to remember the need to physically relax, and to develop courage, I will remember the conditioner *no hurry — no worry*. If I don't hurry, I can't become tense; and worry cannot exist if I am completely relaxed physically.

I believe that the finest way in the world to develop a positive response to pressure, to build self-confidence, and to express purpose is through action, which expresses my love and help to others — right now, this minute. Presto — I eliminate pressure. But I need action, which I get through co-ordinating my goals with my positive mind.

Strong, positive goals are my best prescription for boredom and frustration. I know that once I put a strong goal in my mind, it's like a magnet which draws upon all my resources.

I will be constantly reminded of the basic rules of goal setting by the conditioner *structured goals chart my course.* By this I mean that my goals will be sharply defined, realistic, and challenging. These will be my goals and not someone else's. I will select business goals which are *forcing,* and which *demand* performance with me.

So as to know what I am doing, I will *track* my progress each week and each month. I will also use visualization to *picture* what it would be like to accomplish my forcing goals.

By using the phrase *time is money,* I will be reminded to set a dollar value on my time and to evaluate each function. It will also remind me to arrange each day in an orderly, unhurried manner by listing my tasks for the next day in the order of their priority and by crossing off each job as it is finished.

Through these steps I will build a strong support system for my self-image and my self-esteem. This support system is designed to produce the external rewards I desire in the form of money and recognition, and in the intrinsic feelings of self-worth, a sense of accomplishment, and a *winning* feeling.

Through the conditioner *I become what I think,* I will constantly be reminded to build a mental picture of being successful and positive in what I do. I *see* myself clearly moving toward goals of health, happiness, and success in my business and personal life.

I will constantly increase my vertical competence in my

work through a desire to grow, through dedication to my chosen work, and by the most effective use of my time. By using all these techniques, I can begin to *see* myself at a new level of competence.

I'm proud to be serving, winning, and growing. Through my dedication to the realization of my own potentials, my performance in my life will be relaxed, free flowing, and professional in every regard.

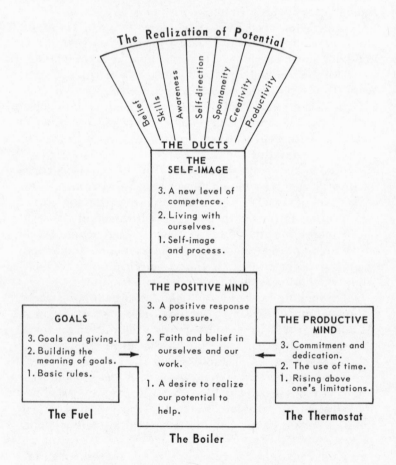

Note: The process of realizing your potential is fun. Above all else, stay loose, enjoy yourself, and smile. You go this way only one time! As the ad says, "Grab with all the gusto you can for it."

Summary

How, then, does a man begin to regulate the intensity of his vertical growth during his career?

It has been suggested that the deeper and more meaningful his involvement is with his career, the more quickly his potential will develop. There can be no question that the man who is enthusiastic, committed, and dedicated attracts success. The point is that, through his attitude, he can consciously develop this powerful force so that it works in his favor instead of against him.

The second regulator of potential is the efficient use of time. The associative phrase "Time is money" is used to recall the need to set a dollar value on each important function, to price-evaluate one's time, and to arrange the day in an orderly, unhurried manner. This has a material impact on the level of competence a man can achieve.

The third component, the ability to be objective, to transcend one's own limitations, is a controllable characteristic which maximizes potential. The success of objectivity is evidenced by a man's ability to act positively rather than constantly react in a negative way to circumstances. The more he acts, the more professional he becomes. A true professional in sports, the arts, or in the business world always maximizes his potential, in part because he maintains a greater degree of self-control than the nonprofessional. He can then transcend at least some of his limitations.

Whether it is Johnny Miller and his golf swing, or a great salesman or manager, there is a recurring need to return to fundamentals. That is what this book is all about, and the programming method is suggested to develop and reinforce the fundamental attitudes necessary to the realization of potential.

At this point in his travel toward realizing potential, a man has reached the end of the line, and to keep from being left there, he continues the round trip each day of his life. If the components of potential viewed on this journey have been successfully used and integrated, he emerges as what is often called a whole man.

6

The whole man

What is a whole man? The dictionary defines wholeness as "not injured, complete, not divided up." In terms of the process of realizing potential, wholeness describes the ultimate extent to which an individual has integrated the mental, physical, and spiritual dimensions of his life. As a man develops and coordinates these three dimensions, he is increasingly able to live more fully and to share himself with those around him. In this context, any man can be whole. The test is not external, although the results of this integration are often clearly recognized, but in the internal fusion of these dimensions of one's life.

The whole man is much more than an achiever. He actualizes his own creativity and uniqueness, and he values the uniqueness of others. His responses to his life situations testify to his integrity, responsibility, and full regard for the dignity and worth of other people. In a nutshell, he is authentic because he knows himself. He is genuine and trustworthy in his individual relationships and as a member of society. He has the courage to assume responsibility for his own actions.

The whole man possesses a personal philosophy which not only is effective when things are good, but also functions well during times of trouble, whether that trouble occurs in his business or his personal life. He has at least a reasonable idea of who he is, where he intends to go, and what his principles are.

Effective Control

One of the most important attributes of a whole man is that he is in control of his life. While he accepts external disciplines, he does not depend on his external environment to protect him. His life is based on a positive attitude and a strong self-concept which rejects the directives from his childhood and the necessity to have his ego nourished by those around him. His concept is instead based on a strong sense of his own identity and his own personal values. Rollo May has defined this attribute essentially as "centers of strength within ourselves which will enable us to stand, despite the confusion and bewilderment around us."

An able executive described his view of wholeness in this way: "A whole man feels himself responsive to the myriad demands on his life. Just giving of yourself is one part of it, but I think there's another part of it too. That's what these different parts of a life give to the other, or give to the whole fabric. What I mean by that is that when I'm out doing a community activity, I find that I'm not just perhaps accomplishing something in the community but I'm tending to gain a perspective on my business life, which gives me a greater balance. In other words, I have guides which tend to put my business in a total perspective. So, really, that's an example of community activities making me a better person.

"My family, the same way. My kids can sit around and take a lot of stuffiness out of me very fast. When one has a balance in his life, one achieves a perspective which allows him to operate the various facets of his life to greater depth, with greater understanding, with greater resiliency. A phrase that ties it all together, it seems to me, says that a guy is working at it, at all these various dimensions of his life, pretty well. Nothing seems to be sort of overtaking him. He doesn't seem to be overcome. He is responding and performing; his health doesn't seem to reflect it negatively, his results are good, and his results appear to come from a balanced reservoir."

This man's achievement index is at about a level of 7½ to 8 vertically and horizontally, and represents a desire for balance in his goals.

Another achiever in business put it differently. He said, "In order for me to grow consistently during my lifetime, I have to constantly reassess my goals, so as to always be an achiever. In this way, a man retains his vigor and vitality. He needs at all times to say, 'I am achieving my goals.' I'm not saying that someone else's goals are my goals, but each man should be achieving against whatever his particular standards are. To me, my major goals are in my work, and I have to be able to say I'm happy in it and my family's happy with it. A man has to enjoy his work. Most of the people I know who are unhappy with their lot do not enjoy their work."

This man scored himself exceptionally high in his business achievement level but, except for his family, rather low in other activities. His composite index rating was still high. His emphasis is almost entirely on his vertical potential.

It would appear that a man who can achieve a composite achievement index at a high level is certainly on the way to at least feeling whole. Every man's individual problem is to structure his goals in such a way that they are fulfilling to him. Again, the mix of his goals can be very much an individual matter, but for most businessmen, and for practical reasons, the emphasis must usually be on strong and satisfying business goals, with potential then spilling over to other aspects of his life. He then uses a coordinated and, in a sense, sequential series of actions which help to determine his own special lifestyle. These actions relate significantly to the production of energy and intellect and the development of a wholesome self-image.

Mind and Body Coordination

Wholeness is also importantly determined by the degree of coordination between the mind and the body. The ability to harmonize the mind and body so that they are integrated and free from imbalance and tensions is the mark of any dedicated professional. For example, a skilled pianist has no need to consciously will his fingers to move; the music flows out of him without effort. When the mind and body are working together in perfect accord and harmony, a person will tend to be whole. To the degree that this coordination does not exist, he loses wholeness and becomes inept and strained, and his performance in life itself can be impaired.

The Potential for Keeping Fit

As previously discussed, mind acts on body and body on mind, and the consequences of malfunctioning of the two in terms of physical and mental illness can be tragic. The ability of a businessman to establish a satisfactory achievement level can be directly related to the state of his physical health. Certainly, the lack of good physical condition impairs to a marked degree the ability to realize potential. It might be said that good physical conditioning is an essential factor in realizing potential. Similarly, good mental structuring is the other side of the coin, and the proper blending of the physical and mental components tends to maximize potential and provide for wholeness. While this chapter deals with the wholeness of the individual as it applies to his overall life-style, the true professional constantly demonstrates the power involved in the coordination of mind and body.

Physical Health

The impact of poor physical condition on the various components in the process of realizing potential cannot be overestimated. How can one rise above one's own problems if one does not feel well? Obviously, we need good physical conditioning and we need to feel well to effectively use, develop, and coordinate all of the factors of potential.

The following brief comments sum up a few of the important thoughts of the experts in the field of physical conditioning.

The basic rule, perhaps more fundamental and real than any other, is the ancient maxim "nothing in excess." It's my opinion that a man who treats his body this way is not likely to harm himself. Each man soon learns from experience what "excess" means. The variance in what is excessive is amusingly documented by an article about Charlie Smith of Barstow, Florida. He lives alone, drinks, and smokes. He says he'd like to stop smoking, but it's a rough habit to break after you've been doing it for 114 years. Charlie is 132 years old.

As for diet, research shows that (except for nutrient value) the kind of food a man eats is not of particular importance, but the amount is; overeating is quite damaging. There is an old saying that "more men have been slain by their suppers than by the sword." There are two specifics a businessman may use with regard to weight control. One is to decrease the quantity of food he eats, and the other is to increase the amount of exercise he takes. Of course, the best way is to do both.

Unfortunately, cigarette smoking is one of the greatest inhibitors of good health in this country. While the damaging effects of smoking have been widely publicized and medical data support the fact that it causes lung cancer, heart disease, emphysema, and a host of other damaging conditions, there is another effect which is rarely discussed. Cigarette smoking is psychologically addictive and makes a person slavish to the point where a man's entire day is structured around a cigarette. It is usually one of the first thoughts that enters his mind in the morning, and he develops a certain pattern throughout the day. (The author is an expert in this field, having been a smoker for many years.) The president of one large corporation told me, "I will have to think long and hard before I promote a man who smokes to an important position in this company. I figure that, in addition to the fact that he may be a future disability case, he has decreased his energy by at least 25 percent because of smoking."

With regard to the need for physical activity, all experts, without exception, recommend exercise. There is dispute about those exercises which are vigorous, such as jogging, but except in extreme physical disability cases, anyone can walk. It is suggested that the businessman walk at a fairly rapid clip, but at the same time have an awareness of his surroundings, so that he makes this exercise an enjoyable one. All forms of sports, of course, are used and can be helpful. The decision as to what a man does is, again, a personal one, but the fact is certain that physical exercise is vital to good physical conditioning.

A word about alcohol, the great American pacifier. For many businessmen, alcohol is the primary method for the release of tension, and indeed it is a most pleasant method of reaching a different level of consciousness. It is, however, a drug, and its use should be subject to the fundamental rule involved in the maintenance of good health, which is "nothing in excess." Unfortunately, alcohol is physically addictive and can therefore be difficult to use in moderation. It can also be psychologically addictive and can easily become a substitute for the use of potential.

Dr. Morris E. Chaffetz, director of the National Institute on Alcohol Abuse, has pointed out that there are nine million alcoholic persons in the country whose illness directly affects forty million members of their families. While alcohol is a poison which affects the brain, nerves, heart, and liver, a most important effect is that it moves quickly to that part of the brain (Freud named it the "superego") which has to do with our behavior and judgment. Because it relaxes this part of the brain, it seems to solve a great many problems. However, there are nine million reasons (the alcoholics) which clearly indicate that alcohol does not solve problems. In terms of a whole man, the excessive intake of alcohol is damaging in the extreme to the physical, mental, and spiritual dimensions of life. It can be deeply inimical to the development of potential.

No one seriously questions the relationship of good physical conditioning and strength and endurance. People who are in good physical condition have fewer complaints, are

definitely more alert, have more energy, and are less likely to
have disease. Michel de Montaigne (1533–1592) remarked,
"Men do not usually die, they kill themselves." In terms of
potential, it would appear that the ultimate physical goal is not
necessarily that of living to age 100, but of extending the
vigorous and productive years.

Mental Health

There are often marked changes in the self-image and
how a man feels about himself when he engages in a physical
conditioning program. This is evidenced by his posture, bearing, increased energy level, and positive outlook. In fact, a
feeling of aliveness, of enjoying living, can be closely related to
being in top physical condition. Consequently, the concept of a
man over age 40 being "over the hill" is beginning to change. It
is being increasingly recognized that the pot belly, waning
sexual and physical powers, and flabbiness are not inevitable.
The medical profession has found that the decline in physical
and mental ability occurs primarily because of disuse and lack
of exercise, and is not a biological programming which insists
that a man is old at 55 or 60.

The maintenance of physical fitness for a businessman
includes the following factors:

It should be fun. Exercise can and should be varied, whether
in the form of games one enjoys, in walking, in swimming, or in
the use of exercise machines and saunas, steambaths, and
massage.

A man should try to develop his own rhythm, which is a relaxed
effort as opposed to a stubborn will to win. While competition
in golf or tennis can be great fun, the businessman should not
forget that he will never be an Arnold Palmer or a Rod Laver.

There should be an awareness by the individual of the impact of a
physical-conditioning program on the realization of total potential and self-fulfillment. An ongoing program of physical
conditioning is one of the finest investments a businessman can
make in his total well-being.

When a man reaches the point of "feeling like a million dollars," he should apply this energy to new areas of his potential. Physical fitness is often accompanied by other self-disciplinary traits which are essential to the process of developing potential. Here are some effective physical-conditioning ideas for the busy businessman:

1. Start the day with a brisk walk, even if only for a few minutes. Renew your vigor by breathing deeply.

2. Relax several times during the day for two to three minutes. Use the relaxation technique: Breathe deeply and slowly; relax your eyes and feel the relaxation descending through your body; count down from 10 to 0 until you feel yourself gradually becoming more deeply relaxed at each count.

3. After working hours, continue with physical activities like golf, tennis, swimming, or any other sport which takes you out of doors.

4. When you are tired, get up from your chair and stretch and stretch. This exercise can be done at any time and will get the kinks out. Breathe slowly and deeply. In Yoga, breathing is called "prana," the life force.

5. In place of the extra highball or coffee, drink juice, which supplies vitamins and minerals.

6. Take frequent breaks and vacations from your routine. It's important to your health and well-being that you separate yourself from the business arena where you are constantly under pressure. The achievement of physical potential is reflected in the old proverb, "What the fool does in the end, the wise man does in the beginning."

The Spiritual Dimension of Potential

The spiritual dimension of potential from a business standpoint is presented on the basis of the here and now and not the hereafter—faith and believe in one's self, in one's family, in one's work, and faith in the decency and integrity of man. It can be difficult to maintain faith when confronted by the hard facts of business life, the incessant pressure for profits, the materialism, the drive for power and prestige.

Faith and Integrity

The news broadcast each day seems to proclaim the breakdown of the integrity and decency of mankind. In a recent commencement address at a high school in Pennsylvania, a senior said, "Can you be surprised that many of us have our doubts about the American system, when the credibility of every President we are old enough to remember has been called into question? Is it any wonder, then, that the style today is not to look forward to the future and to what it may bring, but to yearn for the more carefree (as we like to think) good old days? . . . We have grown up media-blitzed and prematurely old. This is what has happened to the younger generation: [We] have experienced, genuinely or vicariously, an adult life while still children . . . but we accept the challenge."

A fundamental message of the great religions is the need for faith. The Bible says (Matthew 17:20), "If ye have faith . . . nothing shall be impossible unto you." And (Mark 9:23) "If thou canst believe, all things are possible to him that believeth." In modern-day parlance, one might say, "If you want it badly enough, you stand a good chance of getting it." Only recently have we begun to understand that we are innately endowed, goal-striving beings who are meant to live fully and to have a healthy self-image. The tools of visualization, the components of the positive mind, structured goals, and self-image development have always been available. The instructions for attaining this desirable state of being (if *you* have faith, according to *your* faith; if *you* can believe) have been known for centuries, but we have not heeded them. Adherence to these simple instructions is a lonely pursuit. Nobody—a corporation, one's friends, one's associates—can engineer *your* self-fulfillment. But if you take charge of yourself, "all things are possible."

While we have little control over the length of our life, we have much to do with its quality. The Bible and other sacred books advise man to choose life: that is, select a course. This ideal is set forth in all great religions, and its intent is not the acquisition of possessions but creative growth, self-understanding, peace of mind. As a practical businessman engages in realizing his potentials—when he chooses to involve, expand, and continually develop his capabilities—he can discover a never-ending creativity in life. As he shares his capacity to live fully with others, he also increases that capacity for himself.

The basic origin of this message and the beauty of individual growth and use of potential is spiritual in nature.

The Art of Giving

The second aspect of potential, in this context, is that of giving. Frequent reference has been made to the philosophy of giving, and the religions of the world often reflect on the need to give. The golden rule, "Do unto others as you would have them do unto you," expresses the basic human need to give. The Old Testament says, "Thou shalt love thy neighbor as thyself." The problem of interpreting and obeying this injunction lies in the fact that we are indeed selfish and self-centered, that we do indeed love to acquire money, and that businessmen primarily seek to accumulate security during their lifetimes. In recognition of this fact, corporations today have established a wide variety of programs to provide for the financial security of their people during illness, disability, death, and old age. To provide extra cushion, men seek to accumulate funds as supplements to these programs and eventually to pass on as an estate to their children. I cannot remember an achiever who was not also acquisitive.

It would seem that our innate selfishness would make it impossible for us to love our neighbor. Yet a philosophy of giving is a vital activator of potential and, when combined with strong goals, maximizes potential and human relationships.

But giving more than one is expected to give is probably as close to loving our neighbor as most men can aspire to. From the viewpoint of the spiritual dimension of potential, a serving philosophy develops a man's competence, productivity, and sense of inner worth. In this context of "loving his neighbor," a businessman gains wholeness. In broader terms, it would be difficult to imagine Russia and the United States facing each other with enough atomic power to obliterate each country a hundred times over if both sides were to "love" each other enough to give just a little more than they had to.

What could be more spiritual in the world we live in than a corporate policy whose deepest concern was the maximum development of the potential of its people—potential that encompassed the integrity, decency, self-respect, and growth of a whole man? Idealistic? Yes, and not simple to implement. But, as the modern saying goes, "this is where the action is."

Some Characteristics of Wholeness

Richard Bach, in *Jonathan Livingston Seagull,* said, "Look at Fletcher, Lowell, Charles . . . are they all so special and gifted and divine? No more than you are, no more than I am. The only difference, the very only one, is that they have begun to understand what they really are and have begun to practice it."

The Self-Actualized Man

The process of realizing potential provides a series of checkpoints and components, its purpose being to provide the framework of a life plan for self-fulfillment and individual security. In its broad outlines it is applicable to any man, but it can be adapted to an individual's ability to develop his own special creativity and to choose the direction his own life will take.

The components of potential are much like the notes in

the musical scale. They may be used or played as a child plays the piano, or they may be one of the richest experiences of life. Used creatively and with finesse, they can represent the highest form of human expression. Beethoven took the familiar notes of the musical scale and with his genius rearranged them into the Fifth Symphony. The mature man uses the components of potential in an integrated, coordinated way which brings his many potentials into play. He is aware that he is engaged in an ongoing process of growth and that the stakes are high—the well-being of himself and his loved ones. He merges his experience and his intuition into creative decisions which make his life exciting and worthwhile.

The whole man uses goals, directed toward his upward climb, as the primary method of actualizing his creativity. He visualizes, he imagines, he dreams. He creates an environment for the exercise of his creativity. Through his dreams he opens doors which would otherwise remain closed. He retains an open, receptive approach to things and ideas, and reserves judgment. He ceases to listen only to voices which are internalized from his past experiences and from his peers. He experiments and looks for associations and connections between things, no matter how irrelevant they at first seem. He explores before applying his logic. He unshackles his imagination and draws on the creative powers of his subconscious mind. He seeks self-fulfillment through his commitment to action, and his goals are directed toward the development of his potential, both vertically and horizontally. He is an achiever, and he actively seeks the intrinsic and extrinsic rewards of growth. He actualizes his creativity through hard work, alertness, and discipline.

Philosopher Morris Friedman said, "What modern man needs is a ground on which to stand and meet the ever changing realities and absurdities of a tetronic age . . . that might enable us to withstand bureaucratization and surveillance."

In arriving at such a ground on which to stand, the whole man is constantly involved in the process of realizing his potential for living fully. He accentuates every phase of self-realization through belief in himself and in his goals. Businesses and people everywhere are looking for men who have the kind of conviction they will fight for.

A clear call for victory (whether it is on the football field or in a business) from someone in command can turn failure into success. The whole man who is pressing toward success is capitalizing on the power of desire, which brings into play the concentration of his energy. His motivating force is belief in himself and his ability to achieve his goals, and this adds creativity to his hard work.

When a man begins to understand himself, when he begins to search out his potential, he begins to know and practice what he really is and he develops certain characteristics that reveal this growth.

Self-Direction

A whole man is one who has taken charge of his mind. He ceases to be like a ship with no destination, carried by the tides and creaking and groaning when the sea gets rough, becalmed when the weather is fair. His ability to control his actions is based on his purpose, and his motivations are linked to that purpose. He has learned the art of self-motivation, and he has structured his life to accomplish his objective. He has become his own man, responsible for his own destiny and proud in what he is doing with his life. Because he knows himself, he can realize and reach his own potential, and therefore will choose the path he must follow to achieve self-realization.

John Gardner, in his book *Self-Renewal*, says:

Exploration of the full range of his own potential is not something that the self-renewing man leaves to the chances of life. It is something he pursues systematically, or at least avidly, to the end of his days. He looks forward to an endless and unpredictable dialogue between his potentialities and the claims of life—not only the claims he encounters, but the claims he invents. And by potentialities I mean not just skills, but the full range of his capacity for sensing, wondering, learning, understanding, loving and aspiring. *

The whole man seeks to shape his life rather than to be shaped. He rejects a conformity which directs that he become subservient to external events. He adapts to change and is responsive to the ebb and flow of life and to the rapidly moving events which impinge upon him. He retains a sense of freedom, nurtures the opportunity to move into new directions, and avoids the rigidity inherent in the premature leveling-out process. Through self-direction he develops self-respect, responsibility, integrity, and the capacity to adapt to his environment. He rejects a support system which is based on what his company, his associates, or his family can do for him. Yet he uses his creative abilities to relate to those around him in ways which are mutually profitable, and he increases his capacity to share himself with others.

Awareness

Another characteristic of the whole person is his capacity to live fully in the present. A person without a meaningful purpose and without structured goals will tend to live in the past or in the future, and his pleasures come in thinking how happy he will be when he retires, or when he has no college expenses, or when he gets a promotion, or some other future or past experience. His daily activities become automatic, and he becomes less and less aware of the enjoyment and pleasure of the moment he is in right now. A man realizing his potential savors life in the present.

Out of the process of growth emerges the quality of awareness, of the importance of living fully and joyously in the present moment. We need at times to live joyously, to renew the ability to marvel at a sunset or the shape of a leaf or the beauty of a lake, to renew our appreciation and understanding of those with whom we work and live, to listen to the messages

* Harper & Row, 1963, p. 13.

of our body and mind and to know what makes us tense and ashamed or good and proud. An aware person in the process of growth has a pretty good idea of what he is doing and how he feels about it, and is therefore in a position to decide what to do about it. He seeks all the joy and life he can in the present moment.

There is a very practical side to awareness. A business owner recently said to me, "Successful managers must have awareness. You don't shut off your mind. One time I was walking from one part of a plant to another—we were making phosphor bronze—and I saw a coil of wire worth about $200 to $300. As I walked past it, I saw it was dirty and not shiny, as though it had been drawn. I asked the foreman what it was and he said, 'I don't know.' It turned out that it had been there a couple of weeks and was on order but had not been processed—obviously because of the dirt. He had demonstrated a lack of awareness over a period of time and this incident resulted in his being fired. In other words, a man in his conversation or activities during the day can have his brain out of gear."

One of the great barriers to awareness and to communication exists because man is able to think faster than he can speak. The whole man trains himself to slow down his own thoughts and to listen to what someone else is trying to say. He trains himself to become a good listener and to ask penetrating questions which enlarge his understanding, knowledge, and ability to communicate with others.

The whole man tries to live as Gandhi put it when he said, "Learn as if you were to live forever; live as if you were to die tomorrow." He releases his energy and his potential through his capacity to live fully and joyfully right now.

Openness

Another characteristic of wholeness that a man develops is the capacity to be more open, or receptive, to experience, to respond more spontaneously to experience. He becomes less defensive and less rigid in his views and responses, and he is able to recognize evidence in a new situation as it actually is instead of distorting it to fit a pattern he already holds. Thus he is able to deal in a far more realistic way with new problems or experiences. To realize potential, one must learn to live and react spontaneously and to trust himself to do so. Many people fear to let their guard down because they are unsure of what might happen. They could dissipate such fears if they would develop the ability to act spontaneously, and try to free themselves from many archaic, outdated, and restrictive responses. These are important elements in creativity and in the process of growth.

An executive who develops his potential is liberated. He can accept responsibility for his own choices and he rids himself of the compulsion to live a predetermined life-style. Instead, he learns to creatively meet new situations and to explore new ways of thinking, feeling, and responding.

The quality of spontaneousness is to be sought after, for the more it is used the more available it becomes to the individual, and the more a chain reaction is set in motion to tap the reserves of a man's potential. The quality of openness increasingly enables him to take in the facts about a situation as it really is, rather than distort them to fit a pattern which he already holds. In this way he becomes more realistic in meeting new problems and new situations. Through the development of the characteristic of openness a man can begin to drop the defensive masks he has used to face life, and to trust his own basic responses. I have heard many executives say: "Too many men in business will avoid going to point A when they make a decision, even though they know it is correct. They automatically go to point B, C, and D, and then back to point A. They're afraid to trust themselves."

The whole man seeks new forms of recreation, sensations, food, experiences, and innovation in order to expand his capacity. Through his spontaneity, he liberates his potential. He overcomes his tendency to inhibit his emotions because it causes him to be remote and ineffective. He seeks genuine and spontaneous outlets which bring him real pleasure. He injects a quality of freshness into his everyday experience, and he listens to his own feelings while allowing others the freedom to express their feelings. He finds a full measure of joy and pleasure from simple things; he enjoys the change of the seasons, the turning of the leaves, the growth of his children. He expresses his spontaneity through his optimism and enthusiasm. His emphasis is on the accomplishments of others and not on their shortcomings and mistakes. Through his optimism and his recognition of other people's success, he transforms the atmosphere around him from negative to positive. His humor and optimism constitute a potent force which powerfully affects his associates and which actualizes his own creativity.

The Development of Creativity

Creativity is the supreme gift of mankind. It will eventually spur human productivity to greater accomplishment than now exists. If it functions as it is meant to, it develops not only potential but also the qualities of decency, integrity, respect for others, and a desire to help.

The ability to create is a natural part of any businessman. Some men are more creative than others, but the difference is one of degree. The use of any man's creative ability often seems to parallel a vertical achievement index. A below-average vertical index impedes a man's productivity and lifestyle. While some men at this level adapt better than others, the impact of its negative effects is there.

Potential, productivity, and creativity become increasingly available when a man believes in himself and when he begins to take charge of his life. Yet, establishing a vertical score of 7 or above can sometimes be a king-size job, even when a man engages in the process of realizing his potential. In addition to the difficulties of self-motivation, external factors such as poor business conditions or a job whose parameters are rigidly fixed must be reckoned with. Regardless of such factors, creativity is 10 percent inspiration and 90 percent perspiration, so that realizable creativity is hard work. The brilliant concert pianist, for example, spends untold hours of practice before he plays his polished performance.

What is the goal? Is it worth its price? In its ultimate sense, the goal is the development of a whole man who has integrated the mental, physical, and spiritual dimensions of his own special life so that he is both mature and creative. He feels fulfilled and he is enjoying himself. A fine achiever said, "Everything you do you should have fun in. To some that means winning, to others it doesn't. But this is what life is all about." Is it worthwhile to seek happiness, peace of mind, self-fulfillment? Is it worthwhile to seek specific goals and health and a positive response to pressure? Is it worthwhile to grow, to seek self-respect and the love of those around us?

The answers to these questions must be yes, and they lie in an individual's own creativity. The creative man takes the risk of making mistakes. A businessman said to me: "Experience is what you get when you don't get what you want. For example, when I was a salesman I learned most from the sales I didn't make, and when I was wrestling in college I learned from the matches I lost." The most common enemy of creativity and innovation is fear, the fear of making a mistake. Dr. Denton Cooley, the great heart surgeon in Houston, Texas, has this quotation from André Gide alongside a color portrait of his heart transplant team, "Man cannot discover new oceans unless he has the courage to lose sight of the shore." Dr. Cooley has plunged fully into the unchartered waters of heart surgery.

Because of his openness, his awareness, his spontaneousness, a whole man rejects a repetitive, stereotyped life-style which inhibits creativity. While a great part of most jobs is routine procedure, the achiever uses standard performance as a launching pad for his own creativity. For instance, when an attorney prepares a will and trust agreement, at least 90 percent of that document is programmed on a machine. It's the 10 percent that must be creatively tailored to the client, and that's really what the client pays for.

The creative businessman looks forward when he meets a crisis. He seeks to innovate, to explore, and to create new dimensions and opportunities in his work and his life. Because he is creative, he often turns adversity into an advantage. Many of the largest companies in the country have survived only because of the creativity of their founders.

In using effectively the components of potential which have been presented in this book, the creative businessman actualizes his own creativity in many ways, some of which are:

1. Because he seeks to maximize his life, he looks to the integration of the three dimensions of his life, and this actualizes his creativity.
2. He cultivates desire, faith, and belief in himself, and in this way he creates a "seedbed" of personal achievement.
3. He prices-out his time so as to avoid excess amounts of routine activity which can stifle his creativity.
4. He seeks maximum enjoyment out of his job, and in having fun doing his work, he maximizes his creativity.
5. He uses visualization in the development of creative thought.
6. By responding in a positive, optimistic, and courageous way to the pressures of each day, he develops his creativity.
7. The whole man utilizes the magnificent mental and physical capacities which have been bequeathed to him, and he thereby actualizes his creativity.

In short, all of the tools in the process of realizing potential are available to actualize creativity whether a man is a salesman, a middle-management man, or a senior executive.

There are no standard solutions or pat answers to guide each man's search for his own self-fulfillment. As he moves from one phase of his career to another, new problems and challenges must be met, and at times it can be a lonely and difficult road. But when the course is charted on the solid ground of growth, of the productive use of his potentials, when he sees clearly the beauty and the meaning of the gift of potential, he looks forward to the challenge of tomorrow.

Epilogue

It is unlikely that the reader of this book will be able to resist scoring his own level of achievement and appraising his effectiveness in the use of the various components which have been developed. He may also have become curious enough to ask this writer, "What I want to know is how you have scored yourself. Most of what you have to say is based on your observation of successful people, but how have these techniques worked out for you? Have they had value?" The answer is a clear yes!

The motivation and the material for this book developed years ago as a result of a personal crisis. During this period my rating went temporarily from a 7 to a 4 composite index figure.

A golf professional said recently that when he is hitting the ball correctly he looks around and he can't understand why anyone can't hit it properly. He also said that when he is not hitting the ball correctly he looks around and can't see how anyone can possibly hit it correctly. The point, of course, is that once you lose your swing, it is difficult to regain it.

While a similar situation can exist with a life-style, I have found that it is quite practical to renew oneself by going back to the basics. The creative use of the components of potential continues to add new values to my life. I especially notice that the fuller integration of the mental, physical, and spiritual dimensions of life stimulates creativity and productivity.

Scoring Your Achievement Index

How might you score your own personal achievement index? The charts given in this section are guides based on the contents of this book. They are intended as a series of check-points for your own personal use. Your answers will be based on your feelings, attitudes, and beliefs, and are therefore entirely personal judgments, valuable only to you.

It has been suggested that a vertical achievement score of 7 or above is most desirable. The scoring system can aid a man in determining whether a low vertical score is caused by his own lack of use of potential, or whether he feels the scope of his work is not using his potential in spite of his best efforts.

A low score in a particular component can pinpoint an area that needs improvement and which may be negatively affecting every other component.

YOUR VERTICAL ACHIEVEMENT INDEX

Present use of your vertical potential in your work
(Score on the scale of 0–10)

1. Your desire to achieve your potential   _____

2. Faith and belief in yourself and your

    chosen work   _____

3. Ability to respond positively to pressure   _____

4. Setting goals properly   _____

5. Building the meaning of goals   _____

6. Goals and a giving attitude   _____

7. Your own self-image (sense of worth)   _____

8. Your ability to live with yourself   _____

9. Seeing yourself at a new level   _____

10. Your commitment and dedication   _____

11. Your use of time   _____

12. Your ability to rise above yourself   _____

    Total   _____

    Divide total by 12   _____

In scoring your horizontal potential it is suggested that two extra points be given for both the family and physical fitness categories because of their great importance to one's well-being. These four extra points tend to equalize the lesser importance of the other categories. It should be noted that some men who score very high vertically can also develop a high horizontal score which is related to their vertical competence. For example, a very able man in the advertising business has found many horizontal activities which bring him into contact with customers, which has proved highly profitable.

It is very often possible for a man to increase his vertical score through the development of his horizontal potential. For instance, growing family relationships and physical fitness can affect vertical potential favorably. Similar effects can occur when recreational and cultural pursuits contribute to a sense of well-being.

YOUR HORIZONTAL ACHIEVEMENT INDEX

1. Your family   _____

2. Your physical fitness   _____

3. Social and recreational   _____

   (friendships, sports, hobbies, etc.)

4. Cultural   _____

   (reading, theater, orchestra, etc.)

5. Community   _____

   (church, hospital, scouts, etc.)

       Total   _____

       Divide total by 5   _____

Your horizontal achievement index   _____

Add your vertical achievement index   _____

       Divide by 2   _____

Your composite achievement index   _____